Battleground Europe
HAMEL

Capture of Hamel village 4 July 1918 by A. Pearse, War Artist (via Mairie d'Hamel)

Other guides in the Battleground Europe Series:

Walking the Salient *by* Paul Reed
Ypres - Sanctuary Wood and Hooge *by* Nigel Cave
Ypres - Hill 60 *by* Nigel Cave
Ypres - Messines Ridge *by* Peter Oldham
Ypres - Polygon Wood *by* Nigel Cave
Ypres - Passchendaele *by* Nigel Cave
Ypres - Airfields and Airmen *by* Michael O'Connor
Ypres - St Julien *by* Graham Keech

Walking the Somme *by* Paul Reed
Somme - Gommecourt *by* Nigel Cave
Somme - Serre *by* Jack Horsfall & Nigel Cave
Somme - Beaumont Hamel *by* Nigel Cave
Somme - Thiepval *by* Michael Stedman
Somme - La Boisselle *by* Michael Stedman
Somme - Fricourt *by* Michael Stedman
Somme - Carnoy-Montauban *by* Graham Maddocks
Somme - Pozieres *by* Graham Keech
Somme - Courcelette *by* Paul Reed
Somme - Boom Ravine *by* Trevor Pidgeon
Somme - Mametz Wood *by* Michael Renshaw
Somme - Delville Wood *by* Nigel Cave
Somme - Advance to Victory (North) 1918 *by* Michael Stedman
Somme - Flers *by* Trevor Pidgeon
Somme - Bazentin Ridge *by* Edward Hancock and Nigel Cave
Somme - Combles *by* Paul Reed
Somme - Hamel *by* Peter Pedersen

Arras - Vimy Ridge *by* Nigel Cave
Arras - Gavrelle *by* Trevor Tasker and Kyle Tallett
Arras - Bullecourt *by* Graham Keech
Arras - Monchy le Preux *by* Colin Fox

Hindenburg Line *by* Peter Oldham
Hindenburg Line Epehy *by* Bill Mitchinson
Hindenburg Line Riqueval *by* Bill Mitchinson
Hindenburg Line Villers-Plouich *by* Bill Mitchinson
Hindenburg Line - Cambrai, Right Hook *by* Jack Horsfall & Nigel Cave
Hindenburg Line - Saint Quentin *by* Helen McPhail and Philip Guest
Hindenburg Line - Bourlon Wood *by* Jack Horsfall & Nigel Cave

La Bassée - Neuve Chapelle *by* Geoffrey Bridger
Loos - Hohenzollen *by* Andrew Rawson
Loos - Hill 70 *by* Andrew Rawson
Mons *by* Jack Horsfall and Nigel Cave
Accrington Pals Trail *by* William Turner

Poets at War: Wilfred Owen *by* Helen McPhail and Philip Guest
Poets at War: Edmund Blunden *by* Helen McPhail and Philip Guest
Poets at War: Graves & Sassoon *by* Helen McPhail and Philip Guest

Gallipoli *by* Nigel Steel

Walking the Italian Front *by* Francis Mackay
Italy - Asiago *by* Francis Mackay

Verdun *by* Christina Holstein

Boer War - The Relief of Ladysmith *by* Lewis Childs
Boer War - The Siege of Ladysmith *by* Lewis Childs
Boer War - Kimberley *by* Lewis Childs
Isandlwana *by* Ian Knight and Ian Castle
Rorkes Drift *by* Ian Knight and Ian Castle

Wars of the Roses - **Wakefield/ Towton** *by* Philip A. Haigh
English Civil War - **Naseby** *by* Martin Marix Evans, Peter Burton and Michael Westaway
Napoleonic - **Hougoumont** *by* Julian Paget and Derek Saunders
Napoleonic - **Waterloo** *by* Andrew Uffindell and Michael Corum

WW2 Pegasus Bridge/Merville Battery *by* Carl Shilleto
WW2 Utah Beach *by* Carl Shilleto
WW2 Gold Beach *by* Christopher Dunphie & Garry Johnson
WW2 Normandy - Gold Beach Jig *by* Tim Saunders
WW2 Omaha Beach *by* Tim Kilvert-Jones
WW2 Sword Beach *by* Tim Kilvert-Jones
WW2 Hill 112 *by* Tim Saunders
WW2 Normandy - Epsom *by* Tim Saunders
WW2 Normandy - Operation Bluecoat *by* Ian Daglish

WW2 Battle of the Bulge - St Vith *by* Michael Tolhurst
WW2 Battle of the Bulge - Bastogne *by* Michael Tolhurst
WW2 Dunkirk *by* Patrick Wilson
WW2 Calais *by* Jon Cooksey
WW2 Boulogne *by* Jon Cooksey
WW2 Das Reich – **Drive to Normandy** *by* Philip Vickers
WW2 Market Garden - Nijmegen *by* Tim Saunders
WW2 Market Garden - Hell's Highway *by* Tim Saunders
WW2 Market Garden - Arnheim, Oosterbeek *by* Frank Steer
WW2 Market Garden - The Island *by* Tim Saunders
WW2 Channel Islands *by* George Forty

Battleground Europe Series guides under contract for future release:
Stamford Bridge & Hastings *by* Peter Marren
Somme - High Wood *by* Terry Carter
Somme - German Advance 1918 *by* Michael Stedman
Somme - Beaucourt *by* Michael Renshaw
Walking Arras *by* Paul Reed
Gallipoli - Gully Ravine *by* Stephen Chambers
Fromelles *by* Peter Pedersen
WW2 Normandy - Mont Pinçon *by* Eric Hunt
WW2 Market Garden - Arnhem, The Bridge *by* Frank Steer
WW2 Normandy - Falaise *by* Tim Kilvert-Jones
WW2 Walcheren *by* Andrew Rawson

With the continued expansion of the Battleground series a **Battleground Series Club** has been formed to benefit the reader. The purpose of the Club is to keep members informed of new titles and to offer many other reader-benefits. Membership is free and by registering an interest you can help us predict print runs and thus assist us in maintaining the quality and prices at their present levels.

Please call the office 01226 734555, or send your name and address along with a request for more information to:

Battleground Series Club Pen & Sword Books Ltd,
47 Church Street, Barnsley, South Yorkshire S70 2AS

Battleground Europe

HAMEL

Peter Pedersen

Series editor
Nigel Cave

LEO COOPER

To my Father and in loving memory of my Mother

First published in 2003 by
LEO COOPER
an imprint of
Pen & Sword Books Limited
47 Church Street, Barnsley, South Yorkshire S70 2AS

Copyright © Peter Pedersen

ISBN 0 85052 938 7

A CIP catalogue of this book is available
from the British Library

Printed by CPI UK

*For up-to-date information on other titles produced under the Leo Cooper imprint,
please telephone or write to:*

Pen & Sword Books Ltd, FREEPOST, 47 Church Street
Barnsley, South Yorkshire S70 2AS
Telephone 01226 734222

Cover: *Dawn at Hamel, 4 July 1918* by George Bell. (AWM ART 03590)

CONTENTS

Introduction by Series Editor	6
Author's Introduction	8
Acknowledgements	9
Advice to Travellers, Maps	11
How to Use This Book	14
Chapter 1 **Hamel and the Germans**	17
Chapter 2 **Australia Will Be There**	29
Chapter 3 **Preparations**	41
Chapter 4 **To The Blue Line**	69
Chapter 5 **Aftermath**	109
Chapter 6 **Cemeteries and Memorials**	122
Chapter 7 **Battlefield Tours**	129
Bibliography	158
Index	159

Maps and diagrams

1. Area covered by this guide, *pages 18 and 19*
2. German dispositions in the Hamel area, July 1918, *page 25*
3. Infantry dispositions and tank routes, *page 46*
4. Infantry/Tank formations for July 1918 attack, *page 52*
5. Infantry and Barrage Start Lines, *page 54*
6. The attack by 4 Brigade, *page 72*
7. The attack by 13 Battalion, *page 80*
8. The attack by 11 Brigade, *page 83*
9. The attack by 6 Brigade, *page 85*
10. Ammunition and tank supply dumps, *page 96*
11. Diversionary attacks north of the Somme, *page 101*
12. Raid by 55 Battalion, *page 102*
13. The attack by 15 Brigade at Ville-sur-Ancre, *page 104*

Car Tour One, *page 133*
Car Tour Two, *page 142*
Walk One, *page 147*
Walk Two, *page 155*
Walk Three, *page 157*

Introduction by the Series Editor

It is one of the peculiarities of the British that they have a strong tendency to remember their defeats and their setbacks far more than their victories. The exceptions to this 'rule' tend to be battles at sea.

The Great War is no different in this regard. 1918 is almost a closed book to most of the public, apart from the Armistice. Very few seem to be interested in how the Germans were forced to sign up to this unconditional surrender in November 1918, or ask how the Germans had been reduced to this state after their massive gains in the spring and early summer of that same year. Perhaps things might have been different if the ghastly traumas of the Second World War had not followed on so swiftly after the terrible years of 1914-1918.

This British characteristic seems to be shared to some degree with the great Dominions. Canada tends to concentrate on Vimy Ridge (admittedly a success); Australia and New Zealand on Gallipoli. The best efforts of military historians to turn people's attention to the tremendous achievements of the British and Dominion armies in 1918 seem to have made but small impact on national consciousness.

The relatively small action at Hamel on 4th July 1918 is a good example of this; as Peter Pedersen points out, it was the precursor and template for much of what happened on the ground afterwards. Admittedly there is now a massive memorial (erected in 1998) on the key point of the battlefield, largely due to the diligent and persistent efforts of John Laffin. But the importance of the battle is still not clear to the majority of visitors to the Somme, and it suffers from being just that little bit too far away from the 1916 Somme battlefield to fit into the popular Somme tour.

This book, I hope, will attract people southwards, to a beautiful part of the Somme countryside and to where some of the most significant battles of the war were fought, in April and August 1918. It provides an element to the new Memorial that has been missing – a coherent account of the battle, well illustrated by reference to official documents, personal memories, contemporary mapping and well annotated photographs. This is combined with some first rate tours on the ground.

It is works like these, a guide at its best, which helps to explain the problems and achievements of soldiers and airmen at all levels – from senior commanders to the private soldiers.

Hamel was an outstanding example of an all-arms battle, and using troops from Britain and the United States as well as the Australians. It was a tremendous achievement, when at long last the materiel was sufficient – more than sufficient – and the expertise and morale was there to transform it into a war winning combination. The imagination and control of John Monash shines out; but great generals need great soldiers, and in the men of the Australian Corps he found these in plenty.

Nigel Cave
Porta Latina, Rome

AUTHOR'S INTRODUCTION

As the attack at Hamel on the southern bank of the Somme early on 4 July 1918 was over in ninety-three minutes and involved little more than a division, readers can be forgiven for asking why it should be the subject of a Battleground Europe title. Ironically, part of the answer lies in the scale of the assault. It went in on a frontage almost a quarter of that along which the entire Fourth Army attacked on 1 July 1916 at the start of the Somme offensive two years earlier, and took an objective set far deeper. And almost uniquely in that war, the victory cost the attackers fewer casualties than it did the defenders.

Tactically, Hamel (strictly le Hamel) was what soldiers would call an all-arms battle because it involved infantry attacking with tanks and supported by artillery and aircraft. True, none of these arms was a stranger to the rest by 1918 but they had never been brought together in such a successful combination. The battle represented a quantum leap in tactical method that consigned the technique of 1 July 1916 to a bygone age and became a model for the British Expeditionary Force thereafter. In particular, the stroke on 8 August 1918, the German Army's 'black day', was simply Hamel on a larger scale. An understanding of the concept and the plan that emerged from it are crucial for grasping the texture of the attack.

The architect was the relatively new commander of the Australian Corps, Lieutenant General Sir John Monash. A militia officer before the war, he developed a tactical philosophy that rested on the intellectual underpinnings of his civilian profession as an engineer. Besides insisting on the most meticulous preparations to keep the unforeseen at bay, Monash emphasised mechanical resources as the main means of preventing the thin khaki line from foundering when it went over the top. The all-arms nature of Hamel epitomised his approach. Monash emerged as a leading figure in the war and was one of the few generals rarely vilified after it.

Like Monash, the Australians he commanded were an important part of the Hamel story. They were unique and had gained a marked ascendancy over the Germans before the battle. But in trying, albeit briefly, to explain why, I am conscious that their reputation, and sometimes their contribution, on the Western Front, has been questioned in recent years. I have quoted, therefore, from the opinions of those who campaigned alongside them. The Australians themselves were genuinely fulsome in their praise of the officers and men of the

BEF's 5 Tank Brigade and rated highly the Americans who fought at Hamel.

Finally, the battle was not part of a larger operation. The plan can be studied without having to take into account its place within a wider scheme. The execution readily breaks down into battalion and even company actions, all of which can be precisely located on the ground and easily followed. Yet the overall sense of the battle always remains. Casual or enthusiast, anyone interested in the Western Front will find Hamel a rewarding battlefield to visit.

P.A. Pedersen
Sydney, Australia

ACKNOWLEDGEMENTS

I spend much of each year on battlefields around the world and the rest in Sydney on my writing. When I am there, my father's unstinting support means that I can devote myself exclusively to the pen. Dad, this book could not have been completed without you. Thanks!

In France, Jacques Follet and Diane Melloy Follett did more than offer generous hospitality. They drove me wherever I wanted to go in the Hamel/Villers-Bretonneux area and my frequent cries of 'Stop!' proved that their patience is inexhaustible. As French speakers and historians in their own right, they also set up and translated at meetings with the mayor of Hamel, M Stéphane Chevin, and the villagers. M. Chevin and his staff were extremely helpful, especially with period photographs. Anais Bartoux furnished details on accommodation available in the Hamel area. I spent many enjoyable hours walking the ground with my colleague Jon Cooksey and appreciated his perspective as a fellow student of the battle.

No request was too great for the staff of the Australian War Memorial, in particular, Ian Smith, Senior Curator of Official and Private Records; Bill Fogarty, Senior Curator of Photographs, Film and Sound; Jillian Brankin, Image Sales; and Anne-Marie Conde, the Reading Room Manager. Their enthusiasm is inspiring and makes working at that magnificent institution a singular pleasure. Claudia Krebs of the Office of Australian War Graves cheerfully provided information on cemeteries and graves, sometimes at very short notice.

Roni Wilkinson was a source of invaluable advice and unending patience. I am indebted to him more than I can say. I would also like to record the assistance of the Reading Room staff at the Imperial War

Museum and the Public Record Office in London.

Finally, I am indebted to C.E.W. Bean, the Australian Official Historian of the First World War, whose grasp of the Australian Imperial Force and its operations remains unsurpassed; and to John Laffin, who dedicated much of his life to ensuring that the Battle of Hamel did not slip into a historical backwater. Both men may have passed away but their work is well and truly alive.

ADVICE TO TRAVELLERS

Hamel lies across the Somme from Corbie and Sailly-le-Sec. Visitors approaching from Amiens should take the N29 past Villers-Bretonneux and then turn north on to one of the minor roads signposted for the village. Those coming from Albert should leave the ring road at the D42 exit south of the town and follow the D42 past Méaulte and through Morlancourt and Sailly-Laurette before crossing the Somme and turning right onto the D71.

Although the area receives far fewer visitors than the better-known 1916 battlefields over the river, the same considerations apply when going to both. Full personal insurance is strongly recommended. Take an E111 Form, obtainable from your Post Office, for reciprocal medical and hospital cover in France and make sure your tetanus vaccination is current. A basic First Aid kit is advisable. If driving, check that you have appropriate vehicle cover.

The size of the Hamel battlefield will surprise you. At four miles end to end, and eight miles if the diversion on the Ancre is included, it is hardly confined and very exposed. Consequently, you stand a good chance of experiencing first-hand the tendency of Somme weather to pack the four seasons into an hour. Be prepared for all conditions, which means hat, sun cream and a waterproof smock. Most visitors bring a camera but overlook binoculars. They are necessary to take full advantage of the breathtaking panoramas that unfold from the Australian Corps Memorial and the tower of the Australian National Memorial at Villers-Bretonneux, and to pick out the more remote locations. A compass will help you orient the maps in this book to the ground.

As the battlefield walks occasionally utilise farm tracks and the sticking qualities of Somme mud are legendary, good hiking shoes or boots are a must. While walking, carry plenty to drink, particularly in summer, and something to munch on. To make the best use of your time, have a picnic lunch. The banks of the Somme and the Ancre are idyllic locations. Fresh baguettes, cheeses, hams, a tomato and fruit can be can be obtained in any of the villages within the area but you will have to provide your own knife, corkscrew (a Swiss Army Knife has both and a lot more besides!) and plastic mug. If picnics are not for you, try the restaurants in Villers-Bretonneux or Corbie.

You are now fully kitted out and ready to go – after a few last minute instructions. Remember that the area is a farming community. Its people make their living from the soil and they get understandably angry when unthinking visitors tramp across their fields. Stick to the farm tracks and the edges of the fields and, if in doubt, ask. Drivers should be careful not to obstruct agricultural vehicles, which is easy to do on the narrow roads. The goodwill on which all battlefield tourers depend rests on these simple courtesies. As car break-ins are increasing on the Somme, do not become a victim by leaving valuables on view. Lock them out of sight in the boot.

Anyone who has been a soldier will recall the warning about unexploded ammunition given before entering a live fire training area. 'Ammunition is designed to kill you,' it went. 'If you come across any, leave it alone.' Hamel was not a training area, but a battlefield on which 200,000 shells were fired, not counting those the Germans sent the other way. As a good percentage of them were duds, which the ravages of time may well have rendered extremely sensitive, the warning is very relevant today. If you see shells stacked by the road or the odd shell or grenade lying about in the fields or woods, do not touch them. Otherwise you risk becoming the last casualty of this battle.

Housing Australian artefacts from the Western Front, audio-visual displays and a substantial photographic collection, the Anzac Museum in the primary school at 9 Rue Victoria, Villers-Bretonneux, is well worth a visit. Allow enough time to watch *Hamel – The Turning Point*, an hour-long documentary made by the Australian Army in 1994 that incorporates period footage, voiceovers and a commentary by the late John Laffin. The opening hours are 4-6 pm Wednesday to Saturday and 10 am-12 noon on Sundays, or you can arrange a visit outside these times by calling the Mairie (03-22-480306) during office hours.

As a further aid, the Office of Australian War Graves has produced a battlefield tour kit entitled *Villers-Bretonneux to Le Hamel March-July 1918*, which consists of a brief history of the Australians on the Somme during that period, an audio-CD to be played at signposted points of interest, photographs and a map. It provides a good

A dud shell on the Villers-Bretonneux road just outside Hamel. The notice is a copy of the request for collection submitted by the mayor.

introduction to the battle and can be purchased at the Anzac Museum and the Historiale in Péronne. I have also seen the kit in the café in Hamel. Australian readers may want to order direct from the Office of Australian War Graves, PO Box 21, Woden, ACT 2606; tel: (02) 6289 6510. The cost is $A20.

While accommodation is available in Albert and some of the villages surrounding it on the northern side of the Somme, you might wish to stay more locally. The following list of local hotels, inns and bed and breakfasts may be useful.

Hotels
Novotel Amiens Est***, CD 934 Bd Michel Strogoff, 80440 BOVES
    Tel: 33 322 50 42 42; HO396@accor-hotels.com
Campanile**, RN 29, 80440 GLISY
    Tel: 33 322 53 89 89
Hôtel Première Classe* RN 29 Pôle Jules Verne, 80440 GLISY
    Tel: 33 322 46 12 12
B&B, ZAC de l'Arc, Rue JB Delambre, 80330 LONGUEAU
    Tel: 33 322 50 46 46
Les Balladins, ZAC de l'Arc, 80330 LONGUEAU
    Tel: 33 322 53 90 70
Hôtel de la Marine, 6 Place Roger Salengro, 80800 CORBIE
    Tel: 33 322 48 01 51 (Closed weekends)
Hôtel de l'Abbatiale, 9 Place Jean Catelas, 80800 CORBIE
    Tel: 33 322 48 40 48 (Closed Sundays).

Inns
Le Logis du Santerre, 2 Rue Raoul Defruit, 80131 HARBONNIERES
    Tel: 33 322 85 80 17
L'Auberge Fleurie, 1 Rue Notre Dame, 80113 HEILLY
    Tel: 33 322 40 61 04 (closed Sunday evenings)

Bed and Breakfast
Jean Marie Van Den Bosch, 42 Rue Emile Bazin, 80800 AUBIGNY
    Tel: 33 322 48 42 47
Isabelle DESSAINT, 6 Rue de Lamotte, 80170 BAYONVILLERS
    Tel: 33 322 85 85 84
Jean BOUCHE, 1 Rue de L'Abbaye, 80720 MARCELCAVE
    Tel: 33 322 42 35 91
Isabelle LECONTE, 2 Rue du Marais, 80800 RIBEMONT-sur-
    ANCRE   Tel: 33 322 40 65 34; vilcomte@wanadoo.fr

Madeleine GODBERT, 32 Rue d'en Haut 'Les Aires', 80800 RIBEMONT-sur-ANCRE   Tel: 33 322 40 64 94
Guillaume HEBDA, 5 Allée des Aubépines, 80800 VECQUEMONT
   Tel: 33 322 48 29 54

Chalet, Mobile Home Hire (April to end October)
Ferme de Bouzencourt
   80800 LE HAMEL
   Tel: 33 322 96 97 76; maes.bernard @wanadoo.fr

Caravan and Camp Sites (April to end October)
La Source, 7 Rue du Port, 80800 SAILLY LAURETTE
   Tel: 33 686 08 57 98
Les Puits Tournants, 6 Rue du Marais, 80800 SAILLY LE SEC
   Tel: 33 322 76 65 56

For more information contact the Comité Régionale du Tourisme de Picardie, 3 Rue Vincente Auriol, 80000 Amiens; tel: 00 33 32 911015.

MAPS

Field Marshal Slim could have been speaking of Hamel when he famously remarked that the British Army's battles are always at the junction of two or more map sheets. Because Hamel occurred at the junction of four trench maps in the 1:20,000 series, the Australian Corps produced a 'one off' map for the main attack south of the Somme simply entitled La Neuville, Edition 1, on which the British trenches and German trenches were correct as at 16 and 19 June respectively. It does not have a reference number in the top right hand corner and the only example I have been able to find is Monash's personal copy, held in his papers at the Australian War Memorial and marked with the Infantry and Barrage Start and Halt Lines and the Blue Line.

Although I have used the La Neuville map occasionally in this book, obtaining a copy may be difficult unless you contact the Australian War Memorial (02-6243-4211). I strongly suggest that you use the maps on which it was based. Sheet 62dSE, Edition 3A (Local) covers all but the tiny slice of the main battlefield depicted on the adjoining Sheet 62dNE, Edition 3A (Local). Note that Pear Trench is shown as Circular Post. All of the diversions between the Somme and the Ancre fall within the area of the latter map. Sheets 62dSW Edition 2A (Local) and, to a far lesser extent, 62dNW, show the assembly areas and headquarters locations. These maps should be available from the Department of Printed Books at the Imperial War Museum in London (0171-416-5348) or the Western Front Association – if you are a member.

The grid reference system used at the time is still the best way to pinpoint locations on trench maps. They were divided into squares covering an area of 6,000 yards by 6,000 yards. Each was identified by a letter of the alphabet – mainly P in the case of the Hamel battlefield – and further subdivided into six rows of six squares, making a total of 36 consecutively numbered squares each measuring 1,000 by 1,000 yards. Every one of these squares was broken down into four smaller sub-squares that were lettered clockwise as a,b,d,c. The eastings and northings in each sub-square were then subdivided in intervals of ten and marked off thus on two sides. As an example, P.10.a.1.4 was on the main street in the very centre of Hamel. Very accurate references were possible using this system.

You will be surprised at how little the battlefield has changed when the trench maps are compared with the modern IGN Blue Series 1:25,000 maps, which you will need for the driving tours and the walks. The area covered by this guide spreads across Sheets 2408O (Albert), 2409O (Harbonnières), 2308E (Corbie) and 2309E (Moreuil), all of which can be obtained from Waterstone's Booksellers in the UK and the Maison de la Presse shops or major supermarkets in France. You can also order them online from IGN at www.ign.fr.

HOW TO USE THIS BOOK

While the advice might sound gratuitous, start by reading it! By letting the participants, from general to private and the commanders in between, speak for themselves, this guide aims to convey something of what they thought, felt and saw during the origins of the battle, the preparations for it and, above all, the sting of the fighting. The scene set, the next step is to tour the battlefield using the drives and walks suggested in Chapter Seven. Ideally, complete the drives first so that you have a thorough grasp of where all the principal locations are in relation to each other before you undertake the more detailed walks.

The tours will help you relate the maps to the ground and follow the explanations of what it offered to the Australians and the Germans.

Considerations such as fields of fire, observation and keeping direction are constantly mentioned. Make up your own mind about them and about the tactics used. The tactics of individual battalions are frequently described and, quite often, of companies as well.

In the end, it has been said, every battle comes down to the willingness of the infantryman to go forward. More so than the drives, walking the Hamel battlefield will bring you closer to him, to understand his problems, to feel something of his fears. But remember that you will be walking in daylight, whereas much of the fighting took place in darkness made more impenetrable by dense smoke and mist. That difference raises the question of the ultimate purpose of this book.

The soldiers' descriptions are startlingly vivid. Their apprehension as they moved up to the Start Line, the deafening noise and bone-jarring concussion of the barrage, the gruesome spectacle of tanks crushing machine gunners and the terrified looks on the faces of the Germans facing them, the frenzy of infantry combat with bayonet and grenade, the overwhelming sadness at the loss of a comrade held dear and the juxtaposition of humanity with brutality – the soldiers spare nothing. But this book cannot fully bring their words alive. You have to breathe life into them.

Perhaps the best piece of advice I can give you, then, is to use your imagination. You will leave Hamel with more than a technical understanding of the battle. You will have some understanding of what it must have been like to be there. This book will then have fulfilled its aim. It should be your aim on every battlefield you visit.

Prewar Hamel. The church is on the left and the Wolfsberg on the skyline. (via Mairie d'Hamel)

Chapter One

HAMEL AND THE GERMANS

Desperate for victory on the Western Front before the American buildup in France tilted the balance decisively against them, the Germans launched the most spectacular offensive of the First World War on 21 March 1918. Their Second, Seventeenth and Eighteenth Armies fell on the fifty-mile front between Cambrai and La Fère that was held by the Third and Fifth Armies of the British Expeditionary Force. The right of the Third was pushed back but the Fifth Army crumbled. Two days later its exhausted remnants had withdrawn behind the Somme River.

At this stage, General Ludendorff, the First Quartermaster-General and *de facto* Commander-in-Chief, had intended to swing the advance northwest to roll up the British front but hardening resistance around Arras forced a change of plan. Capitalising on the collapse in the Somme valley, he redirected the main thrust towards the railway

March 1918. The Germans attack.

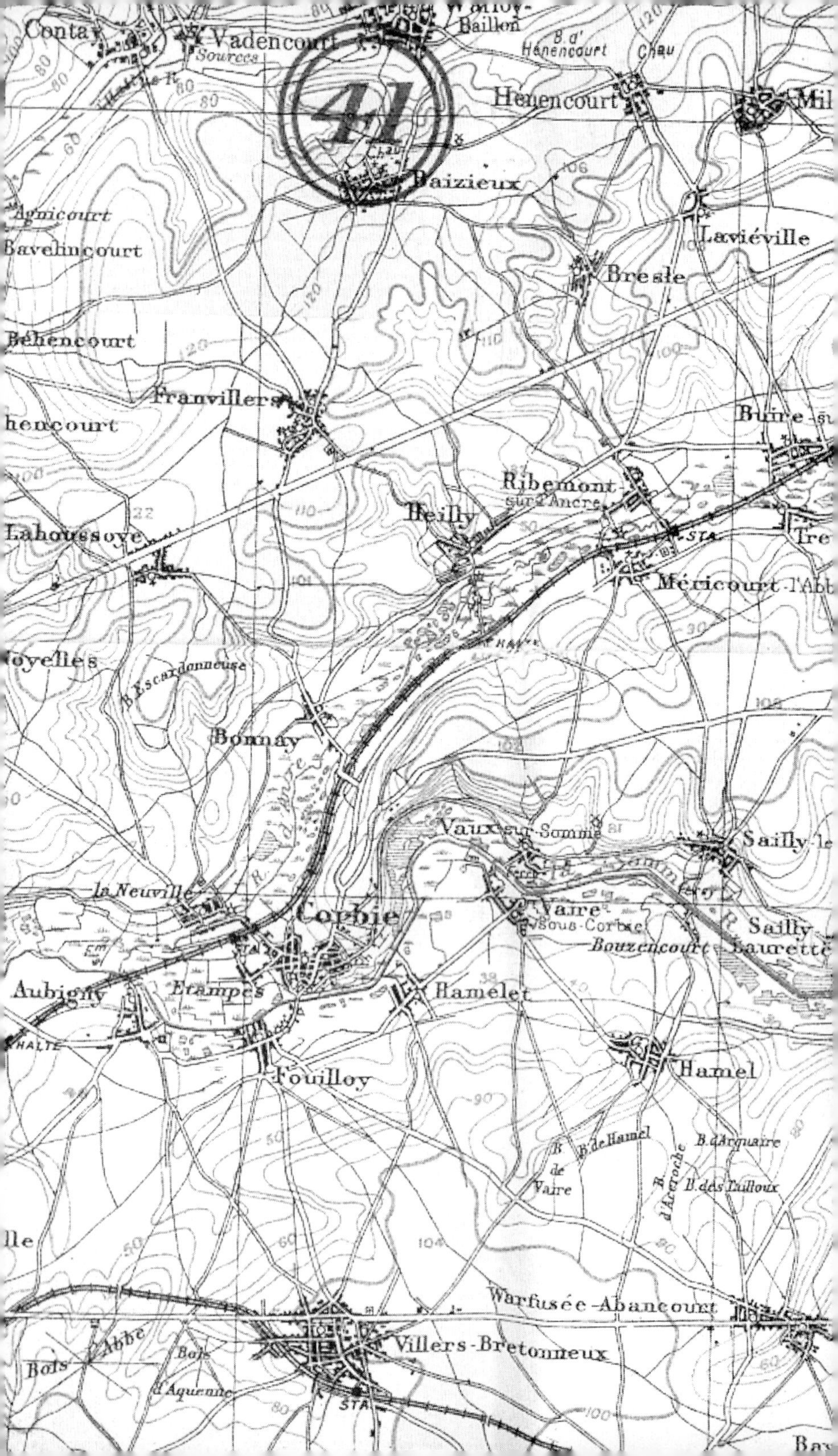

Contay
Vadencourt
Sources
Baillon
B. d' Hénencourt
Chau
Hénencourt
41
Baizieux
Agnicourt
Bavelincourt
Laviéville
Bresle
Béhencourt
Franvillers
hencourt
Buire-su
Ribemont-
sur-l'Ancre
Heilly
Lahoussoye
Méricourt-l'Abb
Tre
Noyelles
B. Escardonneuse
Bonnay
Vaux-sur-Somme
Sailly-le
la Neuville
Corbie
Vaire
-sous-Corbie
Sailly-
Laurette
Bouzencourt
Aubigny
Étampes
Hamelet
HALTE
Fouilloy
Hamel
B. de Hamel
B. d'Arquaire
B de Vaire
B. des Tailloux
lle
Warfusée-Abancourt
Villers-Bretonneux
Bois l'Abbé
Bois d'Aquenne
STA

1. Hamel within the Somme area.

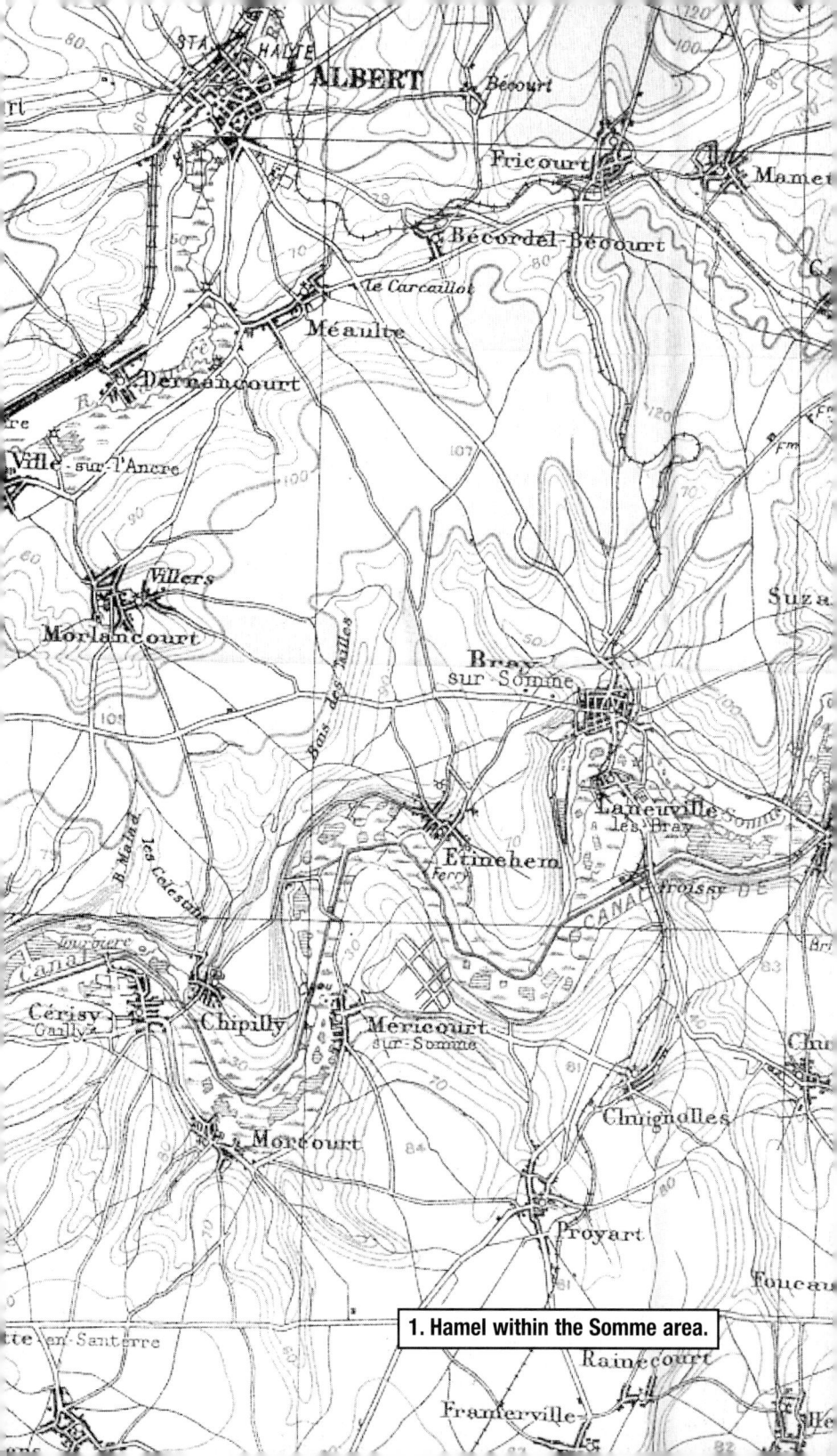

General Sir Henry Rawlinson.

junction at Amiens with the strategic aim of sundering the British from the French. The four Australian divisions sent to the Somme towards the end of March played an important role in stabilizing the line east of Amiens, the key to which was Villers-Bretonneux ten miles to the east. Amiens could be seen from the village, and the Roman Road from St Quentin, now the N29, and the railway from Nesle, both behind the German line, ran through it to the city. The last German attempt to reach Amiens ended when an Australian counterattack ejected them from Villers-Bretonneux on 24 April.

During April, the Australian divisions held the entire seventeen-mile front of General Sir Henry Rawlinson's Fourth Army, which formed the BEF's southern flank. III Corps joined Fourth Army at the end of the month, reducing the Australian line to ten miles. Keeping a division in reserve, they divided it into three divisional sectors. The

Panorama of the German line from Hamel to Vaire Wood taken after the attack. Note the uncut wire in front of Pear Trench (l) and the tanks parked on the terraces (r). (AWM E02833A-D)

northern sector began half a mile beyond the Ancre, crossed the river 1,000 yards west of Ville and extended 1,200 yards south of the Bray-Corbie Road, the modern D1. From there, the central sector leapt the Somme at Sailly-le-Sec, traversed the flats between Vaire-sous-Corbie and Bouzencourt and headed upward onto the Villers-Bretonneux plateau to meet today's D122 from Fouilloy. Crossing the N29 a mile east of Villers-Bretonneux, the southern sector swung over the railway line to Monument Wood immediately south of the village, where the French took over.

The most important part of this line was the stretch south of the Somme, which shielded Amiens. Hill 104, the highest part of the Villers-Bretonneux plateau, arced gently upwards three quarters of a mile northeast of the village, a stone's throw from where the Australian National Memorial now stands. It overlooked Fouilloy, Neuville and Corbie and buttressed the Australian trenches on the spur above the river. The Australians there enjoyed panoramic views eastwards over fields of clover and waist-high wheat to Hamel and the hulking mass of the Wolfsberg above it, crowned today by the Australian Corps Memorial Park, and Hamel and Vaire Woods – Hamel Wood was the eastern end of Vaire Wood. The Germans held all of these features. Skirting Central Copse at the western end of Vaire Wood, their front line, with its redoubts at Pear and Kidney Trenches, followed a sunken road below the Australian line. Except on the Somme flats, the opposing lines were nowhere more than 400 yards apart.

So-called because of its shape, Pear Trench was hidden by the brow

Accroche Wood

of the spur along which the Australian line ran. Behind this shield, it could enfilade attacks towards the Somme or, in the other direction, past Kidney Trench, also eponymously named. As the Germans invariably turned woods into death traps, Hamel and Vaire Woods loomed dangerously. Vaire Trench girded Vaire Wood, which could support the two redoubts. Hun's Walk, a communication trench that started behind Kidney Trench and ran almost 2,000 yards eastwards through both woods to Accroche Wood across a slight dip in the plateau, sheltered arriving reinforcements. Screened on its northern edge by Notamel Wood, Hamel foreshadowed costly village fighting. Towering 260 feet over Hamel, the Wolfsberg added depth to the position and offered artillery observers magnificent all-round views. They could drench the 2,700 yards separating them from the Australians with highly accurate fire.

The hasty defences thrown up by the Germans after their offensive was halted bore no comparison to the elaborate belts of wire, concrete pillboxes and shell-proof dugouts that confronted the Australians on the Somme in 1916 and at Bullecourt and Third Ypres in 1917. Indeed, Ludendorff had initially forbidden any beefing up of the new front line because it would have signalled the closing down of the attack, whereas he wanted to convey the opposite impression to keep his opponents guessing. Some of the trenches in front of Hamel were shallow and silted while the wire, according to patrol information cited in an Australian intelligence summary at the start of July, appeared 'to be hastily improvised and should not afford any great obstacle'.

Hamel Wood   Sunken Road   Hun's Walk   Vaire Wood

Nevertheless, this same report warned that the German 'do nothing' policy was well and truly over:

> Up till recently the enemy has displayed little energy in the construction of forward defences...
>
> During the past few weeks, however, there are increasing indications that he intends to develop a complete two line system with the usual saps, dugouts and communication trenches. In certain areas the work is nearing completion and a considerable defence scheme is evidently contemplated, the tendency being to link up the existing chains of rifle pits and incorporate them in the trench lines.
>
> The only work on rear defences has been on the old French line, which has been cleared out in places and wired. This should prove quite an effective line of resistance when the work is completed. Mined dugouts have been constructed in numerous places in the forward and battery areas, particularly in the sides of embankments for protection against our artillery fire.[1]

Built by the French when they had held this sector, the old French line crossed the Wolfsberg and faced eastwards to protect Amiens. Hampered by labour shortages, the Germans were rushing to prepare it for an attack from the west. The chains of rifle pits were mainly between Vaire Wood and the Roman Road. If the trenches north of Vaire Wood were decrepit, it was because the Germans were concentrating their efforts on key sections of them, such as Pear and Kidney Trenches, both of which bristled with machine guns. Hamel

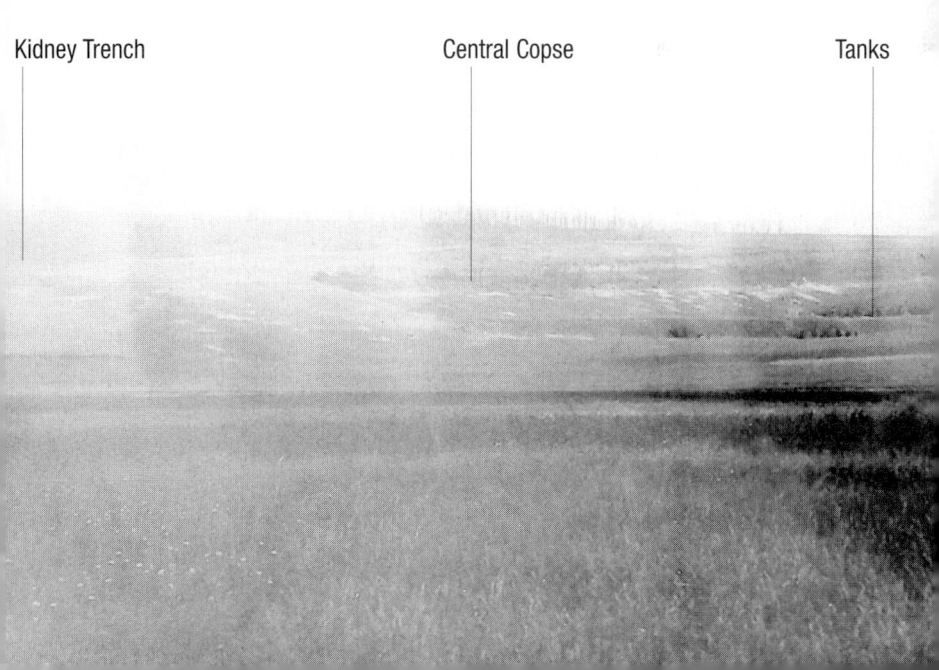

Kidney Trench   Central Copse   Tanks

Pear Trench on the sunken road showing how it enfiladed Hamel (l) and Vaire (r) Woods. (AWM E02705)

Hamel and Vaire Woods and the site of Kidney Trench from the lip of Pear Trench above the sunken road today.

and Vaire Woods were known to be heavily fortified and well defended.

More machine guns lined the terraces, cultivated with fruit trees, which cascaded from Hamel Wood towards Hamel itself. The village had a prewar population of a few hundred, mostly farm workers, whom the German offensive forced to flee. Although the artillery of both sides subsequently destroyed all its buildings, Hamel was not pulverised into brickdust and matchwood as villages in the Somme campaign of 1916 had been. What remained of it was fortified.

The Germans

Owing to the demands of the Spring Offensive, tired and understrength 'trench' divisions occupied this line in April and May.

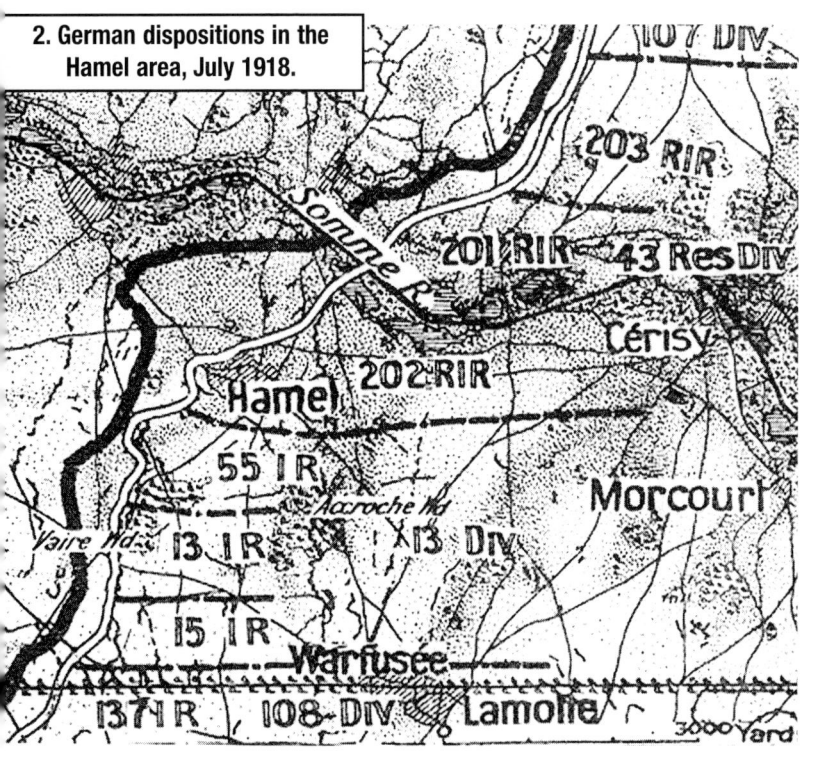

2. German dispositions in the Hamel area, July 1918.

Fresher divisions held it at the end of June. The 107th Division's 52 Reserve Infantry Regiment (RIR) defended immediately south of the Ancre. Garrisoning Hamel, 202 RIR belonged to the 43rd Reserve Division, which deployed astride the Somme after six weeks' rest at Lille. The 13th Infantry Division moved in alongside it after a month's

The most spectacular offensive of the war. German troops move forward.

break near Le Cateau. Its 55 Infantry Regiment (IR) held Pear Trench and the northern part of Vaire Wood, while 13 and 15 IR respectively occupied the rest of Vaire Wood and the line from there to the Roman Road. 137 IR from the 108th Infantry Division took over south of the road. Each regiment kept at least one of its three battalions in reserve. On 22 June the Australians put German strength at 2,790 backed up by a reserve of 2,860. With undermanned companies averaging around fifty rifles, they were, in fact, considerably weaker.[2]

The Australians were very familiar with the 107th and 108th Divisions but uncertain of the effects of the recent fighting on the morale of the other two. The 13th Division, a Westphalian formation, was thought to be

> ...*a division of good quality. During 1915 the Westphalians distinguished themselves by excellent work on defences and fought tenaciously on all occasions. At Verdun and on the Somme, too, the 13th acquitted itself well. Both in 1916 and 1917, however, desertions were not infrequent, these being mostly on the part of Poles and Alsatians, who are found in large numbers in the division. The division received a smashing blow on the Ailette in October 1917 and the drafts required to bring it up to strength again have not been put to the test. It is therefore not possible to estimate the value of the division at the moment.*[3]

This estimate was already dated when it appeared on 3 July. The 13th Division had been in the first echelon during the German offensive and participated in the attack at Dernancourt, the strongest faced by Australians in the war. Its fighting quality on returning to the line after rest was the real question that needed answering but there would be no time to find out. The Germans themselves classed the 13th as a 'first class division'.[4]

The 43rd Reserve Division had opened its account at Ypres in October 1914 and then sent units to Serbia and Russia. The remainder were heavily engaged against the French. In 1916 it reformed as a division and was involved in bitter fighting at Verdun in February and March and on the Chemin des Dames in July and August, and completed two more tours in Russia as well. Returning to the Western Front, it joined the offensive Ludendorff launched in April on the Lys in Flanders. Australian Intelligence concluded:

General Ludendorff, the First Quartermaster-General and *de facto* commander-in-chief of the German Army.

> *Quality.* The 43rd Reserve Division has always been considered a good fighting unit. It is drawn from the depots of guard regiments and consequently contains 'human material' of good quality.
>
> In the end of 1917 it was used as a special counter-attack division. Owing however, to its many engagements and heavy losses, it has frequently been reconstituted.[5]

A contemporary Fourth Army estimate was more forthright, rating the 43rd Reserve as 'an average division' but also adding that it had only been engaged once since March 21.[6]

After spending the first three years of the war in Galicia, the 107th Division arrived on the Western Front just in time to be mauled by the tank attack at Cambrai on 20 November 1917. It advanced on the Somme on 21 March 1918 and fought for another month. After four weeks' rest near Cambrai, the 107th re-entered the line on 16 May at Morlancourt on the Ancre, where the Australians thumped it so badly that it was again withdrawn to the Cambrai rest area. When it returned to the Ancre, the Germans themselves thought that the 107th Division was too battleworn to be relied upon. The Australian judgement was therefore quite accurate:

> <u>Quality.</u> The moral [sic] of the 107th Division is fair but it is not a good fighting division.[7]

The 108th Division was classed as a 'trench' formation. It fought in Russia until the end of 1917 and then against the French in the Vosges before arriving on the Somme in May 1918. The Australians had encountered the 108th from the start of June when it had held the Hamel sector and were able to assess it first hand from prisoners taken:

> <u>Quality.</u> The moral [sic] of the 108th Division is good. As a fighting division it is not of the best as it has spent most of its time on the RUSSIAN front.[8]

Still, the 108th Division's sector on the plateau east of Villers-Bretonneux was devoid of cover and ironing board flat. Australian and French attempts to take Monument and Hangard Woods in similar terrain just south of it in April and May were roughly handled. As the terrain at Hamel was no less difficult, the line south of the Somme remained virtually static for the next two months irrespective of the quality of the German divisions manning it.

NOTES

1. 'Notes on the Enemy Opposite the Corps Front' (Hamel) c. 4 July 1918, AWRS 243/14, AWM; see also J.E. Edmonds, *Military Operations: France and Belgium 1918. III. May-July* (McMillan, 1939), p. 198.
2. C.E.W. Bean, *The Official History of Australia in the War of 1914-1918. VI. The AIF in France During the Allied Offensive, 1918* (Angus & Robertson, 1942), p. 313. Hereafter *OH*; 'Forecast of Available Enemy Infantry', 22 June 1918, Item 361/2, AWM 26.
3. 4th Australian Division Intelligence Summary No. 304, 3 July 1918, Item 1/48, Roll 832, AWM 4.
4. R.A. Beaumont, 'Hamel, 1918: A Study in Military-Political Interaction' in *Military Affairs*, Vol XXXI, No. 1, Spring 1967, p. 11.
5. 'Notes on the Enemy Opposite the Corps Front'.
6. Fourth Army Information Summary No. 189, 25 June 1918, Item 350/6, AWM 26.
7. *OH. VI*, p. 325; 'Notes on the Enemy Opposite the Corps Front'.
8. 'Notes on the Enemy Opposite the Corps Front'.

Chapter Two

AUSTRALIA WILL BE THERE

By the time the guns fell silent, the Australian Imperial Force on the Western Front had acquired a formidable reputation. 'The greatest individual fighter in the war was the Australian', said the Allied Generalissimo, Marshal Foch, in 1919.[1] Looking back over half a century later, Major General Hubert Essame concurred: 'All who fought in it gave the palm for the best infantry of the war to the Australians'.[2] A junior officer at the sharp end of the 8th Division from the 1916 Somme Offensive onwards, Essame had served alongside them. Even the British Official Historian, Brigadier General Sir James Edmonds, contemporary and confidant of the Commander in Chief, Field Marshal Sir Douglas Haig, held that the Australians were, 'We all agree... the finest'.[3]

Figuring prominently in these assessments was the Australians' ascendancy on the battlefield in 1918. Ironically, the year had begun with fears that they might be waning. Employed as shock troops since their arrival in France, they had launched nineteen attacks on the Somme, waded through the 'blood tub' of Bullecourt, fought at Messines and then spearheaded five of the eleven major attacks at Third Ypres in 1917. After that campaign, some confided to the Australian Official Correspondent, later Official Historian, C.E.W. Bean, that they were 'quite happy to let Fritz keep what he's got and shake hands with him'.[4] Brigadier 'Pompey' Elliott, the legendary commander of 15 Brigade, noted: 'They have not the same spirit at all as the old men had. The difficulty once was to restrain their impatience for action – now we find men clearing out to avoid going into the line at all'.[5]

Brigadier H. E. 'Pompey' Elliott.

Elliott's observation was an inevitable consequence of the AIF's standing as an all-volunteer force. Unless recruiting kept pace with losses, the five Australian divisions would increasingly be comprised of veterans who knew that the odds shortened with each battle. The divisions themselves would gradually wither away, a danger recognised at the end of 1916 when conscription seemed the only answer. But the referendum to introduce it was defeated, resulting in a manpower crisis after Third Ypres. Replacing its 38,000 casualties and anticipated future wastage required monthly enlistments of 7,000 but the average was only 2,500. The half-formed 6th Australian Division in England had already been broken up and conscription was again rejected in a second referendum held in December 1917. Paradoxically, then, a decision that capitalised on the manpower shortfalls sent Australian spirits soaring.

The Australian Corps

In June 1916 the Australian Government pressed for the creation of an Australian Army but Haig rightly considered that five or even six divisions were insufficient. Continued lobbying in 1917 culminated in October with a more modest proposal to group the Australian divisions in a single corps instead of the arrangement that split them between I and II ANZAC Corps. Once again Haig demurred, as he thought that a corps of five divisions was too large a command for one man to handle and the system of reliefs within it would be too complex. A corps of four divisions avoided the problem because two could be in the line with the other two ready to relieve them.

When the manpower crisis intervened, General Sir William Birdwood, the Indian Army cavalry officer commanding I ANZAC, and Major General Brudenell White, its Australian Chief of Staff, suggested that the 4th Australian Division, which was the most battleworn, should temporarily become a depot division to supply reinforcements for the others. Besides averting the 4th's breakup, their proposal meant a corps of the magical four divisions and Haig readily agreed. The Australian Corps came into being on 1 November 1917. A few weeks later the 4th Division was rushed into close reserve at Péronne after the German counterstroke at Cambrai, its stint as a depot division over. So the corps consisted in the end of five fighting divisions. With 50,000 non-Australian troops attached, mainly British heavy artillery, labour battalions and American engineers, its strength was 166,000 men, making it the largest corps in the BEF.

General Sir William Birdwood

The creation of the Australian Corps had come as a total surprise and was everywhere greeted with delight. It took full advantage of one of the AIF's major strengths, its homogeneity.

Soldiers from the 2nd Australian Division say hello to Mum!

When three Australian divisions attacked alongside each other for the first time at Third Ypres, their enthusiasm was striking. Watching them beforehand, Bean wrote that they were 'a magnificent combination – all keen to win, keep their reputations and their place in the force'.[6] Afterwards, one commander estimated that the effectiveness of his formation had been increased by a third.

But the strongest influence within the AIF was the mateship in its ranks. Though the closeness of the small group sustained soldiers in every army, in none did it do so more than the Australian. Only veterans of the early days at Gallipoli were given home leave to Australia and, even then, not until September 1918. The rest did without. As the prospect of death or wounding grew more real with each battle, home and the concerns, interests and ambitions that went with it faded to the deepest recesses of a soldier's mind. His platoon and, by extension, company and battalion, filled the void, effectively becoming his family or, as one of them so eloquently put it, 'our father and mother of unforgettable years'.[7] The result was an aggressive spirit, confidence that verged on arrogance and an esprit that could withstand practically any knock.

To the end, the Australian soldier remained 'incorrigibly civilian', accepting the temporary necessity of regulation but never reconciling himself to an existence governed by it.[8] His intelligence, curiosity and initiative unfettered, he was very much a soldier who did reason why. In battle those qualities shone but out of it, helped by pay six times greater than his British counterpart's, he was his own man and became notorious for his indiscipline. This almost schizophrenic contrast made others ambivalent towards him. The size of the Australian military prison population, proportionally ten times larger than the British in 1918, irritated Haig, who blamed it on the Australian government's refusal to sanction capital punishment, but he still counted them among his best troops. Lieutenant Campbell, an English gunner, disliked the Australians for their independence, but was always glad when they were in the line nearby.[9]

Field Marshal Sir Douglas Haig felt that if the Australian government would sanction capital punishment it would make the Australian soldier more controllable.

Into Battle

Four months spent recuperating, refitting and

training at Messines during the mild winter of 1917/18 had given morale another fillip. With few casualties, the flow of returning wounded temporarily eased the manpower shortage. When the German offensive began on 21 March, the Australians could see that this battle would determine the outcome of the war and were very keen to enter it. Over the next month, the 2nd, 3rd, 4th and 5th Australian Divisions scored notable successes at Hébuterne, Dernancourt and especially Villers-Bretonneux, while the 1st Australian Division played an important part in saving Hazebrouck after the Germans struck on the Lys.

Nonetheless, at 15,000 men the cost necessitated the step that had hitherto been resisted. In April, 9 Brigade from the 3rd Division and 12 and 13 Brigades from the 4th each disbanded a battalion to maintain their other three, a reorganisation forced on the British Army two months previously. The co-incidental doubling of the Lewis Guns in each platoon was some compensation – the Australian divisions, like the Canadian, were among the first to receive the extra weapons. But the future was clear. More fighting meant more disbandments. Even if operations were extremely cost effective, the Australian Corps would inevitably decline unless a way of reducing casualties could be found.

In the aftermath of the German offensive, those concerns seemed a long way off. For the first time since their arrival on the Western Front, the Australians were free of the mud and confinement of trench warfare and they revelled in the new conditions. Holding the angle between the Somme and the Ancre, the 3rd Division was delighted to find itself amidst wheat crops and green fields where sheep and cattle grazed. At Hazebrouck, Lieutenant H.V. Chedgey of the 1st Battalion wrote: 'the men are keen and in excellent health... We fight in open fields, among hedges and farm houses'.[10] What was termed 'peaceful penetration' began as patrols used stealth to ambush, cut off posts and take prisoners. Designed to create more room for defence by advancing the line locally, it became a competitive private war that gave free rein to individual initiative, patience and bushcraft. Lieutenant George Mitchell from 48 Battalion led thirteen men on a typical patrol:

> ...we advanced cautiously through a wheat crop, and then crawled through the long grass. There was a little MG fire. A few flares were coming over. We crawled on and on. At length I found a deep comfortable shell hole. A strip of wheat ran along our left a few yards away. Listening we heard coughs, the click of rifle bolts and the sound of picks and shovels. A flare fired from our left dropped almost on our heads. Sergeant Halliday and I

Ville-sur-Ancre. The ground over which the 2nd Australian Division attacked on 19 May 1918.

> *worked forward through the grass. Thirty yards ahead of us was the Hun screen. Behind a large number of men digging furiously. We squirmed back to the rest of the party. I got them ready. We all stood up together and gave rapid fire on to the party in front. 'Bang' a rifle seemed to go off almost in our ears so we switched around and blazed into the crop. Then silence. Not a leaf stirred. We crouched down in our shellhole. Still no answer. So I sent them off in the direction of home.*[11]

Others saw the results of their efforts. On a hot May morning near Morlancourt, Lieutenant A.W. Irvine of 18 Battalion correctly guessed from the stillness in a troublesome machine gun post opposite that the Germans were asleep. Organising a raid in ten minutes, he jogged across No Man's Land with eighteen men and returned in another ten minutes with twenty-two prisoners and the machine gun. The Australians did not fire a shot and suffered no casualties. The Germans were unaware until the evening that their post had gone. Haig wrote of the 3rd Division on 9 May:

> *During the last three days* [they] *advanced their front about a mile... The ground gained was twice as much as they had taken at Messines last June, and they had done it with very small losses; some 15 killed and 80 wounded; and they had taken nearly 300 prisoners.*[12]

During May, formal attacks by the 3rd and then the 2nd Division captured Ville along with more than 150 prisoners from the hapless 107th Division. In the 2nd Division's attack on 19 May, 22 Battalion assaulted the German outpost and front lines in the Little Caterpillar and Big Caterpillar respectively, two sunken roads that head south from the modern D120. Gallipoli veteran Sergeant William Ruthven won the Victoria Cross for saving the situation when the advance, thinly spread on a 1,500-yard frontage, faltered. His citation reads:

> *During the advance Sergeant Ruthven's company suffered numerous casualties, and his company commander was severely wounded. He thereupon assumed command of this portion of the assault, took charge of the company headquarters, and rallied the section in his vicinity. As the leading wave approached its objective, it was subjected to heavy fire from an enemy machine-gun at close range. Without hesitation, he at once sprang out, threw a bomb which landed beside the post, and rushed the position, bayoneting one of the crew and capturing the gun. He then encountered some of the enemy coming out of a shelter. He wounded two, captured six others in the same position, and handed them over to an escort from the leading wave, which had now reached the objective. Sergeant Ruthven then reorganised the men in his vicinity and established a post in the second objective. Observing enemy movement in a sunken road nearby, he, without hesitation and armed only with a revolver, went over the open alone and rushed the position, shooting two enemy who refused to come out of their dugout. He then, single-handed, mopped up this post and captured the whole of the garrison, amounting in all to thirty-two, and kept them until assistance arrived to escort them back to our lines. During the remainder of the day, this gallant non-commissioned officer set a splendid example of leadership, moving up and down his position under fire, supervising consolidation and encouraging his men. Throughout the whole operation he showed the most magnificent courage and determination, inspiring everyone by his fine fighting spirit, his remarkable courage and dashing action.*

William Ruthven VC as a lieutenant.

In June, the 2nd Division reached the edge of Morlancourt, stunning the Germans, who lamented that in a few minutes 'a complete battalion had been wiped out as with a sponge.'[13] South of the Somme, the 4th Division harried the area in front of Hamel and Vaire Wood.

These operations coincided with the final 'Australianisation' of the corps at the end of May. Major Generals Thomas Glasgow and Charles Rosenthal replaced the last senior British commanders in the AIF, Major Generals Harold Walker and Nevill Smyth VC, in charge of the 1st and 2nd Divisions and Major General John Gellibrand took over the 3rd. Major Generals Sinclair-MacLagan and Talbott Hobbs continued to lead the 4th and 5th Divisions. All were Australian or had lived in Australia for many years, except for Sinclair-MacLagan. A British officer, he was nonetheless regarded as an honorary Australian because he had instructed at its military college before the war. In the most significant change, Gellibrand's predecessor and another Australian, Lieutenant General John Monash, assumed command of the Australian Corps when Birdwood, taking White with him, went to the Fifth Army after General Sir Hubert Gough was blamed for the reverse in March and sent home.

Monash The General

Born in Melbourne, Victoria, on June 27, 1865, to Jewish parents from Prussian Poland, Monash had a formidable intellectual capacity. He spoke German fluently, graduated in engineering, arts and law from Melbourne University and became a pioneer of reinforced concrete construction in Australia. Major engineering works gave him experience of large-scale enterprises. Like the big Western Front offensives, they required the organisation, direction and support of labour and the assembly and maintenance of resources. Moreover, the principles guiding Monash the engineer were equally applicable to high command: foresight, flexibility, co-operation, economy, delegation of authority and an awareness of time. Drawing these comparisons together after the war, he reflected that a background such as his was 'far more useful for general applications to new

Lieutenant General Sir John Monash just before taking command of the Australian Corps.

problems than the comparatively narrow training of the professional soldier'.[14]

By 1914, Monash was a wealthy man but his success did not come easily. He had often worked for expenses only, hoping to win lucrative contracts later on. Meanwhile, he battled to support his wife and daughter. This adversity was akin to what Clausewitz called 'the frictions' experienced at every level of wartime command. Overcoming them developed 'robustness' in Monash, 'the ability to withstand the shocks of war' that the great soldier-scholar Field Marshal Wavell put at the top of his list of qualities a successful general must have.

Monash's thirty years of militia service was more serene. Much of it was in a technical arm, the Garrison Artillery. The intimate relationship between technology, the development of modern weapons and the changes they wrought on warfare fascinated him. 'Fighting Machinery', he concluded, had replaced physical force and brute courage. In March 1908, Monash took command of the Victorian section of the fledgling Australian Intelligence Corps, which prepared mobilisation and troop movement plans. As each plan took shape, Monash's ability to conceive it unfolding was evident. He could also visualise the shape of terrain from a map. This power of creative imagination was a priceless asset given the scale of operations on the Western Front. Monash's last prewar appointment was as commander of 13 Infantry Brigade. When war began he took command of 4 Brigade AIF.

At Gallipoli, Monash experienced the soldiers' war first hand because the cramped conditions in the bridgehead meant that headquarters were virtually in the front line. And as his exhausted 4 Brigade, which had initially held the most vulnerable part, responded to call after call during the breakout in August 1915, he learned the limits to which men could be pushed. In the final phase, an attempt to link up with the British at Suvla, he seethed when the plan was changed just before an attack and 4 Brigade, now fewer than 900 strong, lost heavily. From then on he adopted Napoleon's aphorism: 'Order, Counterorder, Disorder', and insisted that once issued, orders should not be modified unless absolutely necessary for the success of the operation.

The 3rd Australian Division, which Monash commanded on the Western Front, had formed in England while the other Australian divisions were fighting on the Somme. Fully aware of the need for a good showing in its first battle, at Messines in June 1917, Monash was

The living crouch with the dead following the attack on Broodseinde by the 3rd Division during the 3rd Battle of Ypres, 1917. General Monash had planned limited penetration of the German lines and took into account the inevitable German response.

meticulous in his planning. Every aspect of the division's role was covered in thirty-six separate instructions. Monash then ran through the plan at a conference attended by commanders and staffs down to battalion level. So as to leave nothing to chance, they concluded only when 'we [had] a perfect mutual understanding among all concerned'.[15]

At Third Ypres, the 3rd Division joined the attack on Broodseinde. As at Messines, the objectives were shallow, so the assaulting infantry could reach them in sufficient strength to defeat German counter-attacks. By setting limited objectives, Monash maintained,

So long as we hold and retain the initiative, we can in this way inflict the maximum of losses when and where we like. It restores

to the offensive the advantages which are natural to the defensive in an unlimited objective.[16]

The objectives laid down for the next attack, on Passchendaele, were the deepest since the offensive began, even though torrential rain had turned the battlefield into a quagmire. Monash had little time to prepare and his request for a postponement was refused. The 3rd Division was battered.

Monash got on extremely well with Haig, the architect of the Ypres offensive. Haig considered Monash 'a clear-headed, determined commander' and, in his diary, gave him perhaps the greatest volume of unmitigated approval of any one man.[17] For his part, Monash's deep respect for the Commander-in-Chief was based on the way he bore his weighty responsibilities for he considered Haig to be 'quite out of his depth' technically.[18] The Western Front confirmed what Monash had realised before the war: that morale, discipline and an offensive spirit alone could not defeat sophisticated military technology. It had to be countered by technology as well. The hard-pressed infantry, he wrote, would benefit most:

[Its] *true role was not to expend itself upon heroic physical effort... but to advance under the maximum possible protection of the maximum possible array of mechanical resources... guns, machine guns, tanks, mortars and aeroplanes... to be relieved as far as possible of the obligation to fight* [its] *way forward.*[19]

Monash's final battle as a divisional commander began shortly after the German offensive opened. Having been directed to move his division to two different locations on 26 March, he was finally ordered at 1 am on 27 March to plug the ten-mile gap that had yawned between the Somme and Ancre Rivers to expose Amiens. With no time for reconnaissance, Monash relied on his ability to visualise ground and a plan unfolding as he dictated his orders from the instructions he had scribbled on three scraps of paper. Bean recalled the episode as showing Monash's 'great powers of grasp and lucid expression at their best – the officers to whom they were read... recognized, with a flash of pride, "the old man's" masterly touch'.[20]

Monash took over the Australian Corps after a prewar civil and military career that was highly relevant to the problems he faced, followed by three years' fighting. Far from being an 'amateur', he was as experienced and battle-hardened as any of his professional counterparts and his ideas on beating the Germans were fully developed. He was also very lucky. The Corps was at its peak, its prestige and morale were soaring and, with a higher proportion of veterans than the rest of the BEF, it had gained an ascendancy over the Germans it was never to lose. At the same time, the drying up of reinforcements threatened its extinction after a few big battles. How to maintain a vigorous offensive nonetheless would be the biggest test of Monash's generalship.

NOTES

1. Cited in H.S Gullett, 'Our Splendid Dead', *Melbourne Herald*, 25 April 1925.
2. H. Essame, *The Battle for Europe 1918* (Charles Scribner's Sons, 1972), pp. 3, 113.
3. Edmonds to Bean, 27 June 1928, Bean Papers, 3DRL/7953, Item 34, AWM.
4. Bean, Diary 95, 30 December 1917, 3DRL/606, AWM (Hereafter Bean, D).
5. Elliott to wife, 31 December 1917, Elliott Papers, 3DRL/3297, Item 6, AWM.
6. Bean, D165, 28 September 1917.
7. G.D. Mitchell, *Backs to the Wall* (Angus & Roberston, 1937), p. 281.
8. *OH. VI*, p. 5.
9. P. J. Campbell, *The Ebb and Flow of Battle* (OUP, 1979), pp. 50-1, 60, 82.
10. Letter dated 23 April 1918, Chedgey Papers, 2DRL/0178, AWM.
11. G.D. Mitchell, D, 27 June 1918, 2DRL/0928, AWM.
12. Haig, D, 9 May 1918, Haig Papers, Acc. 3155, National Library of Scotland.
13. *OH. VI*, p. 240.
14. J. Monash, 'Leadership in War', 30 March 1926, *Monash Papers*, MS 1184, National Library of Australia. Hereafter MP. For Monash's development as a general, see P.A. Pedersen, *Monash as Military Commander*, (Melbourne University Press, 1985).
15. Monash to Major General H.W. Grimwade, 9 December 1916, MP.
16. Monash to Walter Rosenhain, 14 June 1917, MP.
17. Haig, D, 24 May 1917; J. Terraine, Douglas Haig. *The Educated Soldier* (Hutchinson, 1963), p. 215.
18. 'Leadership in War'.
19. J. Monash, *The Australian Victories in France in 1918* (Hutchinson, 1920), p. 96. Hereafter *AV*.
20. *OH. V. The AIF in France During the Main German Offensive, 1918* (Angus & Robertson, 1937), p.177.

Chapter Three

PREPARATIONS

As commander of the 3rd Division, Monash had urged an attack towards Hamel in April to protect his right flank on the northern bank of the Somme from German artillery near Accroche Wood. Rawlinson was also proposing that the 5th Australian Division, then on the southern bank, should seize Hamel as a feint for an Anglo-French attack south of Monument Wood but White objected that it would 'cut up' the 5th at a time when manpower was irreplaceable and the German offensive threat not yet over. When Rawlinson pointed out that the French were making their assault conditional upon the operation, White retorted:

> *If we have to carry out a perfectly valueless attack at the cost of a division which it is earnestly desirable not to waste – there seems to me something very much wrong in our scheme of arrangements.*[1]

The idea lapsed.

When the next German blow struck the French on the Aisne on 27 May, Foch asked Haig to disrupt the movement of their reserves by launching local attacks. In turn, Monash sought proposals from his divisional commanders on 10 June. Sinclair-MacLagan, whose 4th Division held the line immediately south of the Somme, considered capturing Vaire Wood while Gellibrand's 3rd Division on its right attacked across the plateau north of Villers-Bretonneux. Gellibrand was enthusiastic but Sinclair-MacLagan concluded that he would have too few men to consolidate the position. North of the Somme, Rosenthal rejected the only option open to the 2nd Division, another advance along the Bray-Corbie Road. After the recent attacks on Sailly-Laurette and Morlancourt, it was so far ahead of the line on the southern bank that the guns near Accroche Wood were firing into its rear. Any new attack would have to be on the 4th Division's front.

On 13 June, Monash informed Rawlinson that the 'most useful operation' on the Australian front was the one put up by Sinclair-MacLagan, which involved an advance of 1,600 yards over a frontage of 3,500 yards. Six battalions and several days to redeploy the artillery would be needed. Taking Hamel itself would secure more room for the defence of Villers-Bretonneux but require a full division, as White had foreseen in April. Either operation would have met what Monash had been seeking to satisfy the aggressive temper of the Australians: 'a promising enterprise on which to test their offensive power, on a scale larger than we had yet attempted in the year's campaign'.[2] It would also ascertain the state of German morale. Like White, though, Monash judged that the costs might outweigh the gains. He recommended deferment.

Enter The Tanks

Meanwhile Brigadier General A. Courage's 5 Tank Brigade, which was supporting the Fourth Army, completed its re-equipment with the new Mark V tank. At 4.6 m.p.h., it was almost 1 m.p.h. faster than the earlier Mark IV, had more armour protection and, thanks to better insulation for the crew and larger fuel tanks, greater endurance. Needing only one driver instead of four, the tank was much easier to control and, unlike the Mark IV (a breakdown waiting to happen), it was mechanically reliable. Comparing them, the Tank Corps commander, Major General Hugh Elles, wrote that the Mark V was 'as superior to the Mark IV as a 1905 motor-car was superior to one of 1895'.[3] Monash was among the senior commanders to whom he demonstrated it.

Whether Monash convinced Rawlinson or vice versa that an attack on Hamel was possible immediately if tanks were employed will probably never be known. Monash claimed after his visit to Elles that

British cavalry give this Mark V tank more than a second glance on their way up to the front.

he 'resolved to propose an operation for the recapture of Hamel, conditional upon my being supplied with the assistance of tanks, a small increase of my artillery and an addition to my air resources,' and then spoke to Rawlinson.[4] Conversely, Rawlinson wrote on 18 June, 'I went round the Australian Corps today and proposed to Monash and MacLagan an attack with two battalions of tanks against Hamel village and spur to improve our position north of Villers-Bretonneux'.[5] Elles had sent Lieutenant Colonel J.F.C. Fuller, destined to become perhaps the greatest of the tank pioneers, to impress upon Rawlinson the Mark V's potential. Bean suggested that both Monash and Rawlinson conceived the idea simultaneously.[6]

No doubts surrounded the overall suitability of the terrain for tanks. Rosenthal's line north of the Somme secured the left flank. Crowned at the Somme end by Mouse Copse, the spur along which the 4th Division's line ran down to the southern bank blocked the German view of the area immediately behind. It would protect the approach march of both tanks and infantry before they advanced up to 2,700 yards to a final objective line, called the Blue Line, on a frontage that increased from 6,000 to 7,500 yards. Although the steep slopes of the Wolfsberg would tax the tanks, the intervening ground was hard, covered in crops and largely free of shellholes. But the tanks would be vulnerable in Hamel village and Hamel and Vaire Woods. Then as now, tanks do not like built up or wooded areas because they constrain the mobility and manoeuvre on which their effectiveness and security depend.

Partly for that reason, Monash dismissed Accroche Wood as an objective even though it shielded some of the troublesome German guns. More importantly, its capture would necessitate an additional advance of 1,000 yards. Using the analogy of a coiled spring, experience had shown that the further a frontal attack pushed the Germans back, the more it consolidated their resistance. Weakened by the long advance, the attackers reached the objective unable to absorb the shock of the spring when it was released. Monash was adamant: 'This is a limited objective we are going for, and no consideration is going to prompt me to allow exploitation beyond the line chosen. On no account will an attempt be made to go chasing after those guns'.[7] Besides, the Wolfsberg lay between the Somme and Accroche Wood. It gave good observation over the wood and blocked much of the view from the wood over the river.

On 19 June at his headquarters at Bertangles, five miles north of Amiens, Monash briefed Courage, who sent him his plan next day. It

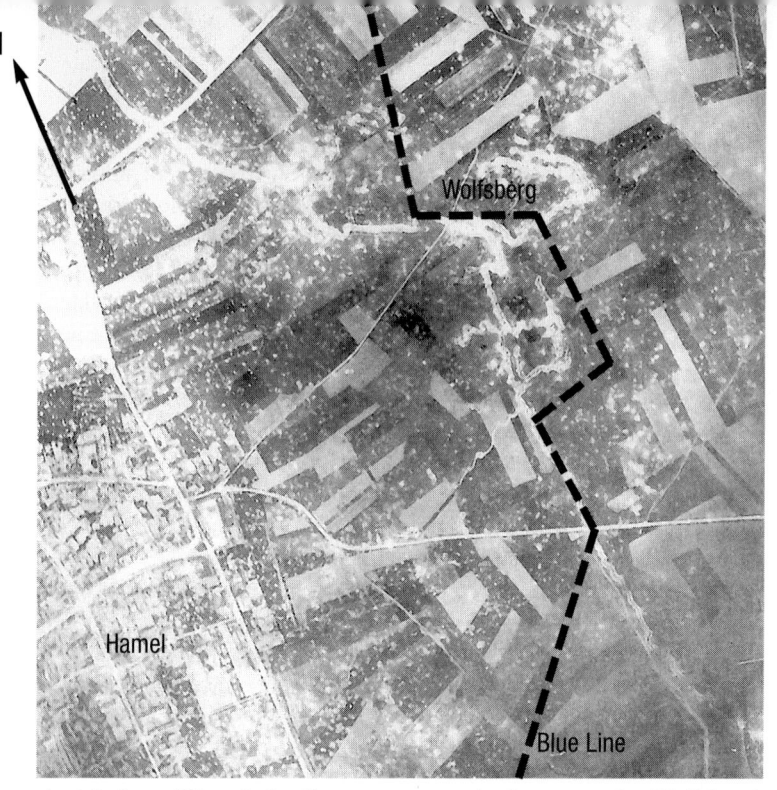

Aerial view of Hamel, the German strongpoint known as the 'Wolfsberg' and the line of the Australian objective – the 'Blue Line'.

was heavily influenced by the initial success at Cambrai on 20 November 1917, when an attack led by 381 tanks penetrated five miles. A tank battalion of three companies plus an extra company, forty-eight tanks in all, would be needed. Courage allocated fifteen tanks to Hamel village, another fifteen to the two woods, twelve to Pear Trench and three to the Villers-Bretonneux flank, leaving three in reserve.

Each grouping was divided into three echelons. The Advanced Section, totalling fifteen tanks, would crush the wire and punch through to the rear of the various objectives to demoralise the Germans, cut off their retreat and block reinforcements. This phase would occur independently and ahead of the twenty-one tanks in the Main Body Section, which were to lead the infantry forward. The nine tanks in the Mopping Up or Reserve Section 300 yards behind them would replace losses and subdue remaining opposition. All but the Advanced Section tanks were to carry ammunition and defence stores for the infantry.

Courage wanted maximum flexibility: 'As the Tanks will have to search ground and subdue targets, there cannot be any fixed interval between Tanks.' All other arms had to conform to the tank's 'chief power', its mobility. Unless the infantry formed up well ahead and latched on to the Main Body Section as it passed them, they might not escape the German barrage and 'the pace of the Mark V Tank cannot be taken advantage of to cover the dangerous zone, without leaving the Infantry too far behind'. The infantry would have to stay in close contact with the tanks 'so that they may at once make good any opportunity the Tanks create and free the Tanks to continue their advance and so keep the battle moving forward by creating a succession of opportunities for the Infantry in rear'.

By crushing the wire for the infantry, the Advance Section removed the need for a preliminary bombardment. Nor would the usual creeping barrage precede the advance as its slow pace and linear shape restricted tank movement. Utilising technical and meteorological advances to eliminate prior ranging, the gunners would fire instead a predicted barrage that 'jumped' between centres of resistance ahead of the tanks and smoke to blind German observation posts on the flanks. Concerned that they might be heard moving up to their start line before the attack, Courage recommended that 'a few aeroplanes with a noisy type of engine should fly above the Tanks and the enemy line in order to drown the noise of the Tank Engine'.[8]

Monash did not alter Courage's concept of the attack as 'primarily a tank operation' in which the infantry role was secondary. As he explained to Rawlinson on 21 June:

The action will be designed on lines to permit of the Tanks effecting the capture of the ground, the roles of the Infantry will be:

(i) to assist in reducing strongpoints and localities
(ii) to 'mop up'
(iii) to consolidate the ground captured.

Like the tanks, the infantry would attack in three echelons. An Assaulting Wave was to escort the Main Body Section and overcome resistance in the village and the woods assisted by a few of its tanks. Twice as strong and following on 200 yards behind, the Supporting Wave would go with the rest of the Main Body tanks to the Blue Line, 'if necessary skirting any centres of resistance which may be holding out', and consolidate it. Acting as carriers, the Reserve Wave of infantry would dump their loads immediately if they were needed to fight.

For tactical reasons and for better command and control, Monash rearranged the objectives. Because Pear Trench in P.8.d could interfere with the attack on Vaire Wood, he grouped both in a Centre Sector whereas Courage had separated them. The Assault Wave battalion escorting the Main Body tanks was to take Vaire Wood, regarded as the main obstacle in the sector, while the two Supporting Wave battalions, having overrun Pear Trench, would follow the tanks to occupy the 1 1/2 mile stretch of Blue Line between P.21.a.4.0 and P.10.d.6.3. A fourth battalion made up the Reserve Wave. One brigade would therefore be responsible for this, the toughest sector, avoiding a messy division of command as there were no obvious features to use as brigade boundaries.

A second brigade would similarly handle the left or northern sector, where the Blue Line extended 1 1/4 miles from P.10.d.6.3 to Bouzencourt. The Assault Wave battalion with the Main Body Section there was to seize Hamel. As the right sector south of Vaire Wood was a bare expanse, the only objective was the Blue Line, which ran from P.25.Central to P.21.a.4.0, just over a mile. But the advance here was awkward, its depth diminishing from over 1,000 yards on the left to 200 yards near the Roman Road. Monash attached more weight to this sector than Courage, allocating it two battalions.[9]

Overall, Monash calculated that the use of tanks would allow him to attack on a frontage of 6,000 yards with ten battalions, of which two formed the reserve. As the Australian battalions averaged around 550 rifles, the density would be less than one man per yard of front for an

3. Infantry dispositions and tank routes.

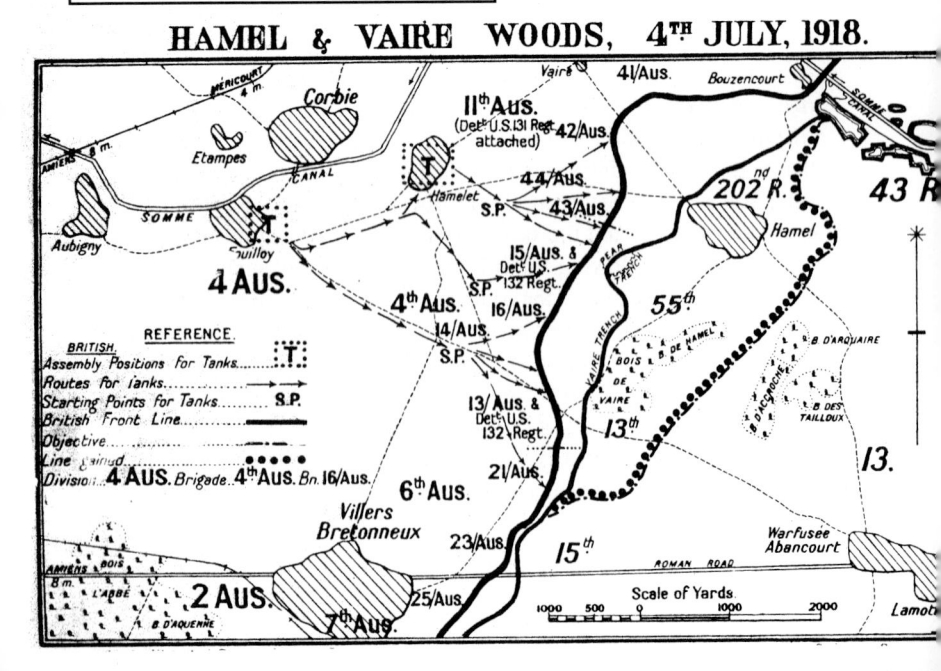

HAMEL & VAIRE WOODS, 4TH JULY, 1918.

advance of well over a mile. Even allowing for the greater strength of positions attacked in earlier campaigns, it was, by their standards, a tiny infantry commitment. At Broodseinde in October 1917, for example, the 3rd Australian Division employed eight battalions to penetrate 1,900 yards on a frontage of 1,000 yards. At Cambrai in November, sixteen brigades had attacked with the tanks on a six-mile front. On the German side, Ludendorff allotted to a division on 21 March 1918 the frontage Monash was giving to each of his battalions.

Monash also opted for a composite attacking force, to be commanded by Sinclair-MacLagan, so that the infantry casualties did not fall entirely on the 4th Division, in whose sector most of the Blue Line lay. Its 4 Brigade, then resting beside the Somme at Aubigny, three miles behind the line, would attack in the centre with 13, 15 and 16 Battalions, and 14 Battalion in the Reserve Wave. Known as an all-states brigade because its units represented every state in the Commonwealth and commanded by Brigadier General C. H. Brand, 4 Brigade was probably the toughest of the Australian formations and two of the AIF's best known and most highly decorated soldiers, Captain Albert Jacka VC, MC and Bar and Lieutenant Colonel Harry Murray, VC, CMG, DSO, DCM, came from its ranks. Monash had been its first commander. The division's other two brigades, 12 and 13, would garrison the newly captured line.

On the southern flank, where the Blue Line ran through the left of the 2nd Division's front, 21 and 23 Battalions from Brigadier General J. Paton's 6 Brigade, a wholly Victorian formation, would assault. Both battalions were also resting on the Somme. The 3rd Division, which had just been relieved by the 2nd at Villers-Bretonneux, would contribute 11 Brigade for the attack on the northern flank. Led by Brigadier General J.H. Cannan, who had commanded 15 Battalion under Monash at Gallipoli, its 42, 43 and 44 Battalions, and 41 Battalion in the Reserve Wave, came from Queensland, South Australia and Western Australia. They were recuperating at Allonville, two miles northeast of Amiens. The Spanish influenza epidemic then raging, combined with severe losses to German gas shelling in May, had reduced 11 Brigade to just on 2,000 all ranks, so that its battalions were below the average strength of 500 rifles.

On 23 June, Monash fixed the date of the attack as 4 July and Rawlinson recommended approval to Haig, remarking that 'the casualties should not be great as it is intended to make the operation a surprise tank attack'. Because of its scale and the risks to security of a postponement, he added that it should not be regarded as one of the minor operations awaiting the green light from Foch.[10] Haig agreed on 25 June.

The Infantry Objects

The high command's enthusiasm was not reflected at the lower levels, which viewed with alarm the elimination of the creeping barrage and the infantry's total reliance on the tanks for protection. Monash had not reckoned on the legacy of the 4th Division's disastrous experience with the earlier Mark 1 tanks at Bullecourt in April 1917. Forced on their account to attack without a creeping barrage, it had been cut to pieces when the mechanically unreliable vehicles failed to arrive on one night and could not reach the German wire on the next. The after action report commented bitterly:

2. Dispensing with the artillery barrage... was unsound. Six of the tanks on which the infantry were entirely dependent for the destruction of the wire were put out of action in a few minutes, leaving the infantry following the tanks with undamaged – and formidable wire – through which they had to force themselves under heavy machine-gun and rifle fire as there was no artillery to keep the defender's heads down.

3. Tanks should be regarded as auxiliary to infantry and not take precedence over them. They should follow the infantry and be used at points where the infantry is held up. ***On no account should tanks replace the artillery function of cutting wire.***[11] *[Author's emphasis]*

On 25 June, the day Haig approved the attack, Brand, Cannan and Paton discussed it with Sinclair-MacLagan at

Major General E. G. Sinclair-MacLagan.

his headquarters at Bussy-les-Daours. Citing Rosenthal's recent success at Morlancourt, which had been achieved conventionally, they overrode Lieutenant Colonel J.D. Bingham of 8 Tank Battalion, who would lead the tanks, and 'decided to carry out operation under a creeping barrage'. Three echelons became two as the now redundant Advanced Section joined the Main Body. The infantry commanders wanted it to move 'as close to front of Infy line as possible, ie as close to barrage as they can safely go. If Infy are held up, tanks move in and replace Arty barrage'.[12] Reluctant to see his arm downgraded, Brigadier General W.A. Coxen, the Australian artillery commander, agreed as did the Corps Chief of Staff, Brigadier General Thomas Blamey, whose appreciation of both arguments concluded:

The Artillery Barrage Method is the more certain. The Tank Method would be more of the nature of an experiment.

The Tank Method offers greater chances of a sweeping success but is somewhat 'chancy'. This might, to a certain extent, be remedied by practice between infantry and tanks.

In view of the fact that the objective is limited, that there is no difficulty as regards ammunition... it is considered that the artillery barrage method is preferable.

Blamey advised Monash privately: 'You can make it an absolute certainty with the artillery – and you can get the artillery lent you for it – so why not make it a certainty?'[13]

Monash always emphasised that a successful commander 'must make the closest study of the psychology of his own troops and must correctly appreciate the influence upon their minds and upon their fighting spirit of all current happenings'.[14] On that basis, overruling Sinclair-MacLagan and his commanders would force them to execute a plan about which they and those they led had serious doubts. Deferring diplomatically, Monash informed Rawlinson on 26 June that the Advanced Section would be done away with entirely, which

...involves a very considerable change throughout. The operation ceases to be primarily a tank operation. It becomes an infantry operation in which the slight infantry power receives a considerable accession by the addition of a large body of tanks.

It becomes necessary to cover the advance of the main body tanks and infantry by an artillery barrage moving at normal infantry rates.[15]

Rawlinson approved immediately. As the Tank Jumping Off Line just east of Mouse Copse was 800 yards behind the Infantry Start Line and tests showed the tanks needed eight minutes to go that far, they were to

Monash and the Australian Corps Staff. Brigadier Generals T.A. Blamey (centre) and W.A. Coxen (right)

move forward eight minutes before zero hour. Once the tanks caught up they were to pass through the infantry and keep station in front of them and as close to the barrage as possible. The tank commanders vainly protested that shells falling even slightly short would hit their machines, which stood almost nine feet high. One tank would be struck in this way. Monash rebuffed a second objection by directing that, 'The infantry commander on the spot is responsible for the joint action of tanks and infantry. He will give such orders to the Tank Section Commander as the situation demands'.[16] Both principles were new and Monash praised Courage for his loyal acceptance of them.

Sinclair-MacLagan received strict instructions from Monash as well. Despite the retarding effect of the creeping barrage, the object was still to establish the infantry on the Blue Line as quickly as possible by having those battalions and tanks not tasked with the capture of the woods and village move around them, link up and then head directly for it. If serious opposition survived the barrage, the infantry were not to deal with it but lie down and let the tanks clear the way. Zero hour was set for 3.10 am, when the breaking dawn would give the infantry and tanks just enough light to see their objectives and each other while the Germans, looking westward, were still shrouded in darkness.

Monash asked for, and got, extra tanks. Two companies of 13 Tank Battalion augmented Bingham's 8 Tank Battalion, making sixty tanks in all. Of the forty-eight in the Main Body, 11 Brigade was allotted twenty-one. Six of these were to replace the six used in the attack on Hamel village for the final assault on the Blue Line. Twelve tanks would go with 4 Brigade in the centre, six to help clear Hamel and Vaire Woods and the rest to protect the flanks of the infantry passing either side. The six tanks with 6 Brigade would head straight for the Blue Line. Another six supported the 'liaison' platoon linking 4 and 11 Brigades and three were detailed for the assault on Pear Trench. Divided evenly between both brigades, the twelve tanks in the Mopping Up Section, renamed the Support Section, formed a reserve. Four of No. 1 Gun Carrier Company's Mark V Star supply tanks would bring up stores and ammunition.

From concentration areas northeast of Amiens near Blangy Tronville, the tank battalions would move to an assembly area around Aubigny by 4 am on 2 July, and that evening to forward assembly areas in the Somme villages of Fouilloy and Hamelet. They were hidden in ruined houses and in the orchards that still surround all three places. Courage set up his advanced headquarters just behind the line on the northern bank in an old windmill, which has long since gone, at J.27.a. On high ground west of Wellcome Wood, called Vaux Wood today, above Vaux-sur-Somme, it commanded excellent views along the frontage of the attack and was equipped with wireless in addition to the usual telephones.

The artillery's expanded role meant that it had to be reinforced well beyond the four field artillery brigades Monash originally sought. He obtained eleven extra brigades which, when added to the eighteen Australian field artillery brigades, yielded 326 guns or howitzers. Four heavy artillery brigades joined the nine already in the corps, making 313 heavy guns available. Some 200 of these would deluge the German artillery on the corps front, estimated at 247 field guns and 130 heavies, with counterbattery fire at zero hour, while the remainder engaged concentration areas and routes for counterattackers and reserves. Monash also arranged for the heavy guns of III Corps and the French First Army to neutralise respectively the German guns north of the Somme and Ancre on the left and those around Marcelcave and

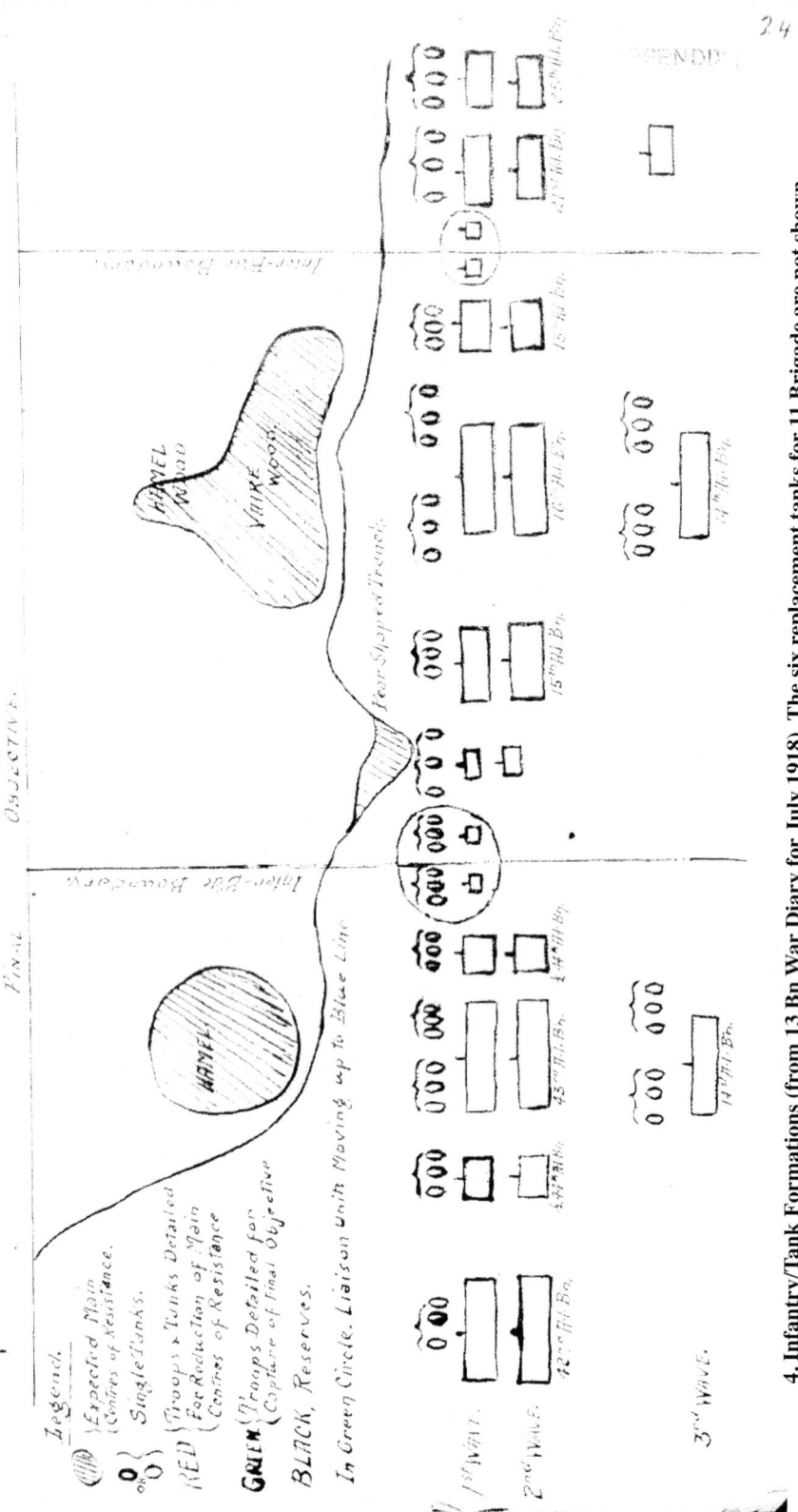

4. Infantry/Tank Formations (from 13 Bn War Diary for July 1918). The six replacement tanks for 11 Brigade are not shown. Note the error '14st A.I. Bn' instead of 41st A.I. Bn in the Third Wave.

Australian 18-pounder battery in action.

Wiencourt on the right, and for a railway gun to pound the communication node at Cappy.

Three belts of fire made up the creeping barrage, starting with 18-pounders shelling 200 yards east of the Infantry Start Line, 4.5-inch howitzers firing 200 yards beyond them and 6-, 8- and 9.2-inch howitzers 200 yards further still. After remaining stationary for the first four minutes to allow the infantry and tanks to edge up to the line of exploding shells, it was to lift 100 yards every three minutes. At zero plus 31 minutes when it would be falling on the eastern half of Hamel, the barrage was to halt for ten minutes so that the battalions destined for the Blue Line could get into position. From then until the Blue Line was reached, zero plus 85 minutes, it would advance 100 yards every four minutes, finally coming to rest on a Protective Barrage Line 400 yards further east and remaining there for the next 38 minutes to cover the consolidation.

One tenth of the ammunition in the barrage was smoke shell, turning Courage's request for a screen on the flanks into one along the entire corps front. On the left flank, which was overlooked by the heights above the Somme, it would be laid at three levels to blind the Germans at every altitude. Although the smoke was to last two hours,

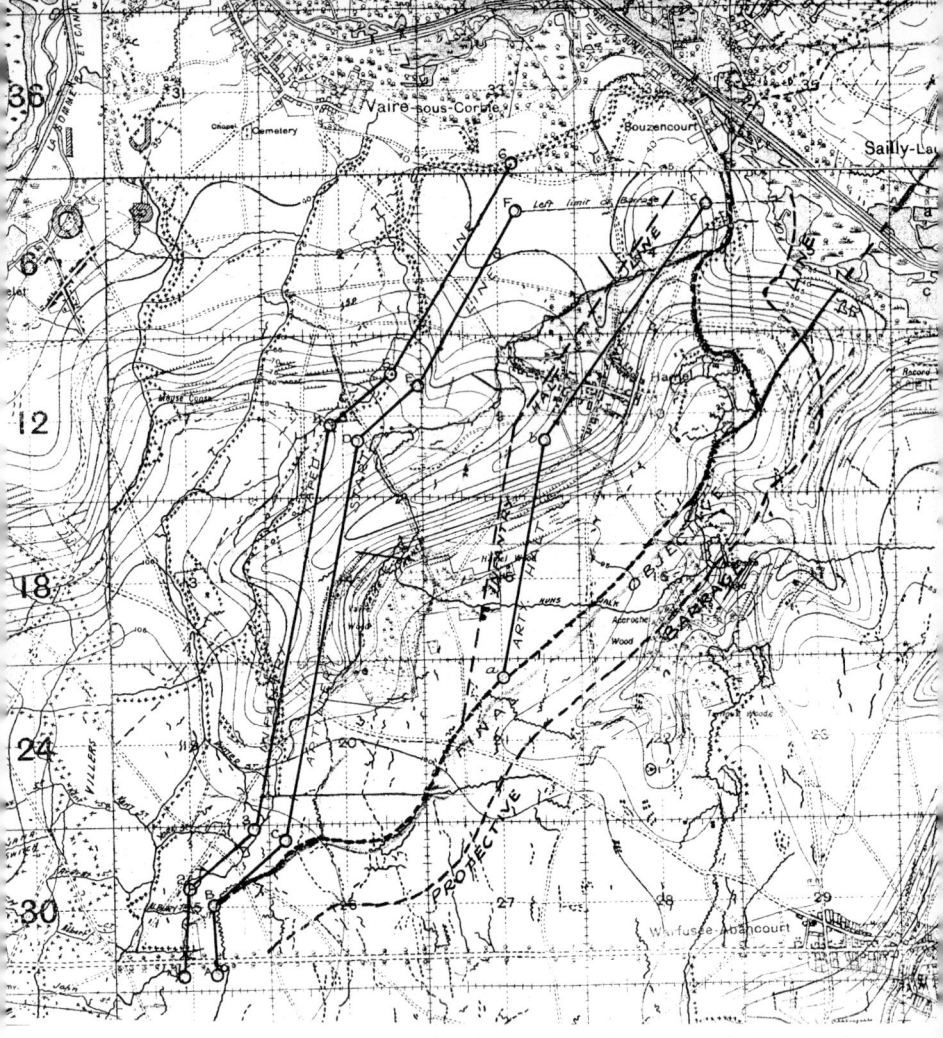

5. The Infantry and Barrage Start Lines, the Infantry and Artillery Halt Lines and the Blue Line (From Trench Map La Neuville, Ed. 1, 19 June 1918).

6 Brigade on the right would still be vulnerable when it cleared as they had to dig in on the exposed plateau. Monash doubted whether they could get down by daylight, when sniping from Accroche Wood would inevitably commence, and proposed a novel use of artillery to solve the problem. A 9.2-inch battery was to fire desultorily on the area beforehand and the shell holes mapped so that the infantry knew where they were.

Monash further directed that virtually all the Vickers machine guns apart from those supporting each attacking brigade were to supplement the artillery with their own barrage. Many of the 111 machine guns used for this purpose were deployed on the northern bank, where they could fire in enfilade across the front of the advance. Nor was this all. Rawlinson asked Haig for a squadron of Handley Page heavy bombers to strike villages and woods behind the German line where reserves might be quartered. From zero hour onwards, aircraft from 5 Brigade of the Royal Air Force were to be over the line ready to strafe counterattacks, while others bombed headquarters and horse lines.

Copying the technique used by the Germans on the Lys and the Aisne, No. 9 Squadron would begin shuttling from Poulainville airfield near Bertangles after daybreak to parachute ammunition onto five drop zones or wherever the infantry displayed a white V-signal. Each of its twelve R.E.8's carried two 1,200-round boxes on a release mechanism designed by Captain L.J. Wackett, temporarily commanding No. 3 Squadron, Australian Flying Corps. He would become a postwar pioneer of aviation in Australia.

R.E.8.

No. 3 Squadron was designated to fly 'contact patrols', the usual means of keeping commanders informed about the progress of an attack. When the squadron's R.E.8's flew low over the battlefield sounding klaxon horns, the infantry were to light matches or red flares in the cover of trenches or shell holes. Maps marked with their positions would then be dropped at Monash's and Sinclair-Maclagan's headquarters. The Australians nicknamed these low-flying aircraft criss-crossing their advance 'Strike a Light' patrols.

More Help for the Infantry

Monash stressed that 'every effort should be made to mystify and mislead as to the point of the attack and the scope of the operation'.[17] Diversions on the flanks would conceal the main front. In the 5th Division's sector on the left, Elliott intended to capture the German line beyond Ville from K.1.b.9.2. to the Ancre, a distance of 1,200 yards, while 55 Battalion from 14 Brigade raided two trenches near the Brick Beacon (K.20.a.7.4), a prominent height named after a tall brick chimney, and raised and lowered papier-maché figures in a dummy or 'Chinese' attack above Sailly-Laurette at K.25.c.5.7. Instead of raiding,

Brigadier General E.A. Wisdom of 7 Brigade on the right preferred to link up with the extremity of the main attack at P.25.b.3.0 by advancing 25 Battalion's line from P.25.c.7.0. to P.25.d.2.4. The creeping barrage would assist these operations and be extended along their fronts by III Corps and the French, a distance of fifteen miles.

The artillery was one of the main agents of deception before the attack. Monash knew that the Germans were aware of British uncertainty as to whether their offensive had run its course, so he ordered a daily predawn harassing bombardment, a routine precaution when an attack was expected, from 26 June. Beginning at 3.02 am to mask the sound of the tank move forward, it included 'flavoured smoke', a combination of gas and smoke that drilled the Germans into wearing their gas masks whenever they saw smoke. As smoke only would be used in the attack, the Australians could assault without gas masks and catch the Germans in theirs. The harassing fire did not engage known gun positions to avoid giving the Germans a reason to move them. They were recorded instead. If a battery moved nonetheless, its old position was occasionally shelled to make the Germans believe that the new one had not been detected.

In order to cover the length of the advance, the field artillery had to be moved forward but without alerting the Germans. A few guns were redeployed early so that target registration data could be obtained but the rest moved on the nights of 1 and 2 July except for the last two guns in each battery, which carried on the harassing programme and arrived on the last night. Ammunition and stores were also brought up under cover of darkness and, like the guns, camouflaged under netting by dawn. The roads had to be clear by then and the pontoon bridge built for the gunners over the Somme between Vaux and Vaire dismantled. A dummy bridge remained to draw fire from the real crossings until the commander of a nearby battery, angry that German shelling was endangering his guns, demolished it. Aerial photography of the German line ceased after 29 June.

To make sure that the Germans saw no signs of a big buildup, first light brought an aircraft from 3 Squadron on a 'police patrol' over the Australian lines to report on anything that might be visible to German pilots. The task of drowning out the noise of the tanks when they left their assembly areas for the Jumping Off Line fell to the ancient but suitably deafening FE2b's from 101 Squadron. From 27 June they began flying 'noise patrols' over the German line from dusk to dawn, dropping flares as though looking for signs of an impending attack. They were to drop twenty-five pound bombs on Hamel and its surrounds on the night of 3 July to mask the sound further. When the tanks left the Jumping Off Line, their clatter would also be covered by the harassing bombardment.

Secrecy went hand in hand with deception. The infantry brigadiers were only told of the operation at their meeting with Sinclair-Maclagan on 25 June. As the activity increased around them, the soldiers knew what was coming but were left to guess the details. Lieutenant Edgar Rule MC, MM of C Company, 14 Battalion, found out towards the end of the month:

FE2b.

One day I sent my boys down to the baths under my sergeant. When the sergeant came back, he pushed his head into my dugout and said: 'Do you know there is a big stunt on, and we are in it? The place is lousy with guns of all sizes back on the river, and tanks are hidden all over the shop'.

This was the first I knew of anything being in the wind; whenever we see tanks, we begin to put two and two together... Our boys are pretty quick at sizing things up, and they'd seen too many of these preliminary preparations to be fooled. Anyway, the cat was out of the bag, and we had to make the best of it. We got our platoons together, and for the benefit of the young soldiers explained the necessity for silence. Once this news got into the front line, there was always the danger of the Hun raiding and capturing prisoners, and then our secret would be his also.

Lieutenant Edgar Rule.

Even now the men were not told what was going on. All they knew was that there was a heavy concentration of guns at the rear.

To minimise the risk from a German raid, orders were not issued in the assault battalions until they had been withdrawn from the line. As late as 2 July, battalion orders stated only that the attack would be carried out 'on a day and an hour to be fixed hereafter'. Commanding officers, such as twenty-three year old Lieutenant Colonel D.G. Marks of 13 Battalion, were not given zero hour until 6 pm the evening before.[18]

As Monash wanted as little as possible committed to paper, conferences assumed a new importance. Attendances increased gradually as the development of the plan brought in commanders and staffs from other branches and services. Twenty-five officers were present at the final meeting on 30 June, which lasted four and a half hours. Monash's agenda listed 133 separate items, from the equipment of the assaulting troops and their relief after the battle to the arrangements for spare Lewis guns and water supply. He could have been describing his pre-Messines conference as he explained to Rawlinson:

> The underlying principle... was that everybody that mattered was present, and had to explain his plans and proposals; and that, when there was any conflict or doubt or difference of opinion, a final and unalterable decision was given, there and then, and no subsequent 'fiddling' with the plan was permitted.[19]

On 1 July, Haig called on Monash and spent an hour going through the plan with him. He thought Monash 'a most thorough and capable commander who thinks out every detail of any operation and leaves nothing to chance. I was greatly impressed with his arrangements'. Monash found Haig 'affability, courtesy and consideration personified'.[20]

The Yanks Are Coming

Just before Monash and Courage started the planning, five American divisions began training in the BEF's rear. General John Pershing, the Commander-in-Chief of the American Expeditionary Force, had allowed the attachment of his raw divisions to the British and French for instruction but wanted the Americans to have their own front instead of being used to strengthen British and French formations. Nevertheless, the continuing worry of another German offensive led Haig to ask him to move two of the divisions, the 27th and 33rd, close to emergency defensive positions behind the Third and Fourth Armies respectively. Pershing agreed, whereupon Rawlinson hit on the idea of using troops from the 33rd Division, a National Guard outfit from Illinois whose 65 Brigade was attached to the Australians, to swell the Australian battalions in the Hamel attack under the pretext of giving them an opportunity to gain valuable experience.

Americans of the 33rd (Illinois) Division with Australians from the 3rd Division, to which they were attached in June 1918. Here they are seen resting at Corbie, 3 July, on their way up to the line.

Monash asked Rawlinson for 2,000 men and confirmed with him July 4, American Independence Day, as the date of the operation to make the proposal more attractive. Rawlinson gained Haig's approval but neither consulted Pershing. The divisional commander, Major General G. Bell, and his superior, Major General G.W. Read of II Corps, were enthusiastic but do not appear to have informed Pershing either. From 29 June, ten companies from the 131 and 132 Regiments of the 33rd Division's 66 Brigade joined the ten Australian battalions, one company to each. The American companies were found to be almost as strong as some of the battalions, which was embarrassing and made for an unwieldy unit. In a neat solution that helped each side get to know the other better, they were divided up into their platoons and one platoon allocated to each Australian company.

The Americans were big men who reminded the Australians wistfully of themselves at the start of the war. Bean wrote on encountering them: 'We felt today as though we had been walking among ghosts. Wherever one goes one is struck more and more by [their] likeness to the men of the old 1st (Aust) Divn at Mena Camp and behind the lines in Gallipoli.' Though some had only been in

France for a few weeks and most had never heard an incoming bullet or shell, they lacked the brashness of their sons in the next war. When a typically sarcastic Australian asked an American: 'Are you going to win the war for us?' he replied, 'Well, we hope we'll fight like you'.[21]

Lieutenant Colonel Joseph Sanborn, commander of 131 Regiment, wrote of the attachment to the Australians: 'From the first when our soldiers came in contact with them they mixed well and took kindly to each other.' The warmth was reciprocated. H.S. Shapcott spoke for 42 Battalion when he found the Americans to be 'very fine chaps, ready and eager to learn and not above taking advice.' In 14 Battalion, Lieutenant Rule was glad to have them on board:

> *On the afternoon of 2 July a bunch of Yanks came up to be distributed among us for this fight. Twelve were put in each platoon, and believe me they were some men. This was the first time that they had been in the line and they were dead eager; and apart from that it bucked our lads up wonderfully. All the novelty of the war had long since vanished for our boys; they had seen too many shows like this, and, as a rule, before such a fight one now sees only set grim faces, but on this occasion everyone was smiling or laughing. They were on their mettle, and were*

Americans moving up to join the Australians for the attack (AWM E02694)

determined to let the Yanks see what the Aussies were capable of.

The Yanks were out for information and our boys were very willing teachers, and it speaks well for the future to see one set so eager to learn and the other so willing to teach. These Yanks view things just the same as we do, and their general trend of ideas was very sensible indeed. They were all men in the prime of life; and such a mixture – one could see among them all the nations under the sun. Yet here they were, citizens of the great republic, with only one idea in their heads. When their names were called, I could hardly keep from laughing, and I felt very grateful to my boys that they had not inflicted such names on my roll book. I heard our C.O. say to one of their sergeants: 'I wish we had some of those Austrians in front of us,' and we got the shock of our lives when he quite calmly replied: 'You know, I was born in Austria, and my father was a Pole.'[22]

Joyriding with Tanks

When the Americans joined them, the Australian battalions were rotating through 5 Tank Brigade's training ground at Vaux-en-Amienois, a village in a quiet valley just outside Amiens. Each battalion worked with the tanks alongside which it would attack. The tanks demonstrated that they could manoeuvre in any direction, were as fast as running infantry and impervious to the armour-piercing ammunition their crews invited the Australians to fire at them. To talk to the tank commander, the Australians were told 'Just ring the back-door bell' by tugging on the rope at the back of the tank. Beginning with the barrage represented by a line of men carrying flags,

Set-piece manoeuvre exercises on the scale of a battalion were designed and rehearsed over and over again; red flags marked enemy machine gun posts; real wire entanglements were laid out to show how easily the Tanks could mow them down; real trenches were dug for the Tanks to leap and straddle and search with fire; real rifle grenades were fired by the Infantry to indicate to the Tanks the enemy strong points which were molesting and impeding their advance. The Tanks would throw themselves upon these places and, pirouetting round and round, would blot them out, much as a man's heel would crush a scorpion.

A red, white and blue flag on the tank meant that it was coming out of action; a red and yellow one that it had broken down. A helmet on a bayonet signified that tanks were needed. The Australians' greatest worry, that a tank might accidentally run over a wounded soldier in the crops, was addressed by having a soldier guide each fighting tank and three accompanying every reserve tank. Soldiers near the wounded man were to stick his rifle in the ground alongside him and tie white tape to the crops so that the tank could see his position. These measures worked wonderfully well. Besides ensuring that no wounded men were crushed during the attack, they greatly helped the stretcher-bearers looking for them afterwards.

The tank crews kept 'open house', taking the infantry for joyrides and allowing them to drive. Exposed to the noise, heat, choking fumes and jolting movement inside the tanks, the Australians experienced the dreadful conditions under which they operated. The junior commanders from both arms 'argued each other to a standstill' on every contentious issue. After 1 July, the tank officers moved into the battalion bivouacs to deepen the friendship and mutual understanding. The result went a long way towards exorcising the demons of Bullecourt:

> *The fame of the Tanks, and all the wonderful things they could do, spread rapidly throughout the Corps. The 'digger' took the Tank to his heart, and ever after, each tank was given a pet name by the Company of Infantry which it served in battle, a name which was kept chalked on its iron sides, together with a panegyric commentary upon its prowess.*[23]

Monash's 'conference habit' was spreading as the brigades and battalions worked through detailed agenda at lengthy meetings with the tank, flying corps, artillery, machine gun, and other officers who would be supporting them. As the attack drew closer, maps showing the German trenches, the objectives and barrage lifts, together with corresponding aerial photographs, were issued as far down as corporals, a wider distribution than in any previous battle. The infantry 'bombed up' on 2 July, each man carrying 220 rounds of ammunition, two grenades, three sandbags, rations for two days, extra water, a pick or shovel and perhaps wire cutters or a flare. Officers carried an SOS rocket to call down artillery in case of trouble. Tank support had clearly made no difference to the infantryman's load!

The Australian Prime Minister, William Morris Hughes, and his deputy, Sir Joseph Cook, called on the Corps that afternoon while on their way to a meeting of the Allied Supreme War Council in Paris. When Monash told them that the men they were seeing would shortly be going into action, the firebrand Hughes was suddenly and uncharacteristically humbled. Bean described a memorable scene as

Australian Prime Minister William Morris Hughes addresses the troops before the battle. (AWM E02651)

the Prime Minister left most of the talking to Cook:

> Hughes, as often as not, lay at full length on the ground, looking into the faces of the soldiers and chewing a stalk of grass. He seemed wrapped up in the men, and was gazing into their faces all the time. I suppose that he was thinking to himself: 'Within thirty-six hours these men will be out there advancing under the bursting shells, going straight into the thresh of the machine-guns... and here they are laughing at Joe's old jokes, wrapped up in his speech as if they were at a picnic'. [24]

While Hughes dined with Monash at Bertangles afterwards, the roads were crowded with vehicles and troops moving forward. Covered by the noise of the FE2bs, the tanks motored into their hides in Fouilloy and Hamelet. A wagon broke down on the pontoon bridge over the Somme, causing a terrible traffic jam until it was pushed over the side. The three attacking battalions of 11 Brigade entered the line in their sector adjacent to the river, relieving two battalions from 12 and 13 Brigades, while 41 Battalion took up its reserve position in the support line behind Mouse Copse. 'It was a glorious night and the scents of the flowers and the growing crops helped to make the march up seem unreal', H. S. Shapcott recalled.[25]

On the right, 21 and 23 Battalions occupied trenches vacated by 5 Brigade. In the centre, Brand feared overcrowding and sent only half of 4 Brigade up. The rest would arrive on the following night and move straight into the attack. Worried about gas, the Americans slept fitfully and rose early on 3 July to get their first look at the German positions, exasperating the Australians who understood that the deception plan required them to lie low throughout the day. Some well directed German shelling quickly convinced the Americans to join them. Soon after, Monash was flabbergasted to receive an order to pull more than half of the Americans out.

Last Minute Hitches

At the same time Hughes had visited Monash, Pershing called on II Corps and was stunned to find that 2,000 Americans, ostensibly attached to the Fourth Army for training, were about to take part in a set-piece attack with the Australians. He immediately told Read that they should not participate. Rawlinson informed Haig, who ordered them withdrawn. The Americans had arrived in two contingents, an initial group of four companies and a second of six, and both Read and Rawlinson thought the direction applied only to the latter. Deeply disappointed and with deep sympathy from the Australians, they left after nightfall on 3 July following some hasty readjustments to the traffic plan that kept the roads clear for the move of the rest of 4 Brigade and the remaining guns and stores.

Meanwhile, at 4 pm on 3 July, Monash learned that the original four companies also had to come out. Meeting Rawlinson at 4th Division Headquarters at 5 pm, Monash told him flatly that it was too late to comply and that if the Americans did not participate, he would call the attack off. In that case, no Australian would fight beside an American again. Unless he had a decision by 6.30 pm, the latest by which cancellation orders could be issued if they were to reach the assault battalions in time, the attack would go ahead. A distraught Rawlinson claimed that he might be sent home if it did not, whereupon Monash replied that keeping the confidence of the Americans and the Australians in each other was more important than preserving even an Army Commander.

Rawlinson directed that if contrary orders were not received from Haig by the cutoff time – later extended to 7 pm – the operation was to continue. While he waited, Monash gave a remarkable press briefing that betrayed not the slightest hint of the tension or the pressure he was feeling. Bean was moved to write:

> There is no question that the old man gave us, as always, a very able discourse indeed. Very few men could have done it. He stood up at his desk there so as to get at the map, and gave it to us without a note – names of battalions and everything . . . The thing has been planned with a thoroughness like that which went before Messines – every particle of the plan, down to the action of companies, being known to the corps commander.[26]

Haig's response arrived with a few minutes to spare. The improvement of the position before Amiens was so important that the attack must go ahead even if the American companies could not be withdrawn before zero hour. Anticipating a long day ahead, Monash went to bed early.

As the drama played out behind them and a heavy fog rose from the Somme, the battalions learned at 6 pm that zero hour would be at 3.10 am. 101 Squadron's FE2bs began bombing at 10 pm, each of its pilots flying at least three shuttles from Poulainville airfield. Searchlights and anti-aircraft fire probed for them as they dropped 350 25-lb bombs on targets illuminated by parachute flares in the hours that followed. At 10.30 pm the tanks left Fouilloy and Hamelet. Passing 4 Brigade's battle headquarters in a roadside quarry at O.12.b.9.5 just outside Hamelet, they idled along tapes that guided them to their positions on

An FE2b about to take off on a night bombing sortie.

4 Brigade's battle headquarters just outside Hamelet. (AWM E02683)

the Jumping Off Line a mile away, which they reached between 11.45 pm and 1.15 am. Thanks to 101 Squadron no-one heard them, but hearts leapt into mouths when a flare, dropped too far westwards, revealed the assembling tanks in light as bright as day for the two minutes it took to float down. Nothing happened.

Half a mile ahead of the tanks, infantry parties cleared exit lanes through the wire, while the battalion intelligence officers supervised engineers in the laying of tape to indicate the Infantry Start Line, in some places out in No Man's Land 300 yards beyond the front trench. The creeping barrage would begin parallel to it 200 yards further out. At midnight, many men were given a second hot meal, which impressed the Americans, and the rear companies from 4 Brigade began arriving. All along the line, the companies in the Assault and Supporting Waves filed out of the trenches and onto their tapes. Each man received a tot of rum and waited.

So did Coxen, sitting by the telephone in his office at Bertangles:

Glancing out of the window I could just discern in the dim morning light the figure of a person slowly pacing up and down the gravel drive in front of the chateau. The figure was that of Sir John... Every now and again he would pause and look at his watch, awaiting zero hour.[27]

Bertangles chateau, Australian Corps Headquarters.

The night was remarkably quiet, making the anxiety palpable. Lieutenant Rule silently asked himself the familiar questions that crossed the mind of every infantryman lying on the damp grass or crop:

> *What luck this time? Who would get it in the neck?... Did the Hun know we were going to attack? Did he know the time? Was he waiting? What sort of barrage would he put down? Could we get beyond it before it fell?*[28]

NOTES

1. Bean, D113, 30 May 1918.
2. *AV*, pp. 43-4.
3. Elles to GHQ, 'Defensive and Offensive Use of Tanks', 3 January 1918, Item 481/8, AWM 26.
4. *AV*, p. 44.
5. Rawlinson in F.B. Maurice (Ed.), *The Life of Lord Rawlinson of Trent* (Cassell, 1928), p. 221.
6. C.E.W. Bean, *Anzac to Amiens*, (AWM, 1968), pp. 459-60.
7. Bean, D116, 3 July 1918.
8. Courage to Monash, 20 June 1918, Monash Collection, 3DRL/2316, AWM. Hereafter MC: 'Tank Corps HQ, 'Characteristics of the Mark V, Mark V Star and Medium A Tanks', 27 June 1918, Blamey Papers, 3DRL/6643, AWM.
9. Monash (S/4761 and Notes) to Fourth Army, 21 June 1918, MC.
10. Fourth Army 190(G) to GHQ, 23 June 1918, Item 350/5, AWM 26.
11. 'Lessons Learned from the Attack on the Hindenburg Line by the Fourth Division on 11 April 1917', c. 30 April 1917, AWRS 979/12, AWM.
12. 'Notes for 4 Div Conference', 25 June 1918, Item 408/4, AWM 26.
13. Blamey, 'Pros and Cons of Tank Method', c. 25 June 1918, Item 361/2, AWM 26; Bean, D116, 7 July 1918.
14. Monash to Foster, 14 September 1918, MP.
15. Monash S4671/1 to Fourth Army, 26 June 1918, Item 361/2, AWM.
16. Australian Corps S/4730 to Attacking Formations, 1 July 1918, Item 361/3, AWM 26.
17. 'Capture of Hamel and Hamel Ridge' Australian Corps Preliminary Report, 4 July 1918, Item 361/3, AWM 26.
18. E.J. Rule, *Jacka's Mob* (Angus & Robertson, 1933), pp. 299-8. 16 Bn Order 67, 2 July 1918, Appendix 34 to 16 Battalion War D, July 1918, Item 23/33, Roll 49, AWM 4; T.A. White, *The Fighting Thirteenth* (Tyrell's, 1934), p. 143.
19. Pedersen, *Monash*, p. 230; Monash to Rawlinson, 5 July 1918, MP.
20. Cited in Terraine, Haig, p.448; F.M. Cutlack (ed), *War Letters of General Monash* (Angus & Robertson, 1934), p. 250.
21. *OH. VI*, pp. 260, 262; Bean, D116, 4 July 1918.
22. *OH.VI*, p. 259; H.S. Shapcott, *War Babies* (MSS 1369, AWM), p. 186; Rule, op. cit., pp. 298-9.
23. *AV*, pp. 49-50; J. Laffin, *The Battle of Hamel* (Kangaroo Press, 1999), pp. 61-2, 116.
24. Bean, D116, 7 July 1918.
25. Shapcott, *War Babies*, p. 189.
26. Bean, D116, 3 July 1918. See also *AV*, pp. 53-4.
27. Coxen to *Reveille*, 12 April 1937, Bean Papers, 3DRL/8054, Item 108, AWM.
28. Rule, op. cit., pp. 301-2.

Chapter Four

TO THE BLUE LINE

As the racket from 101 Squadron continued, the tanks started their engines at 2.59 am. Three minutes later the harassing fire began and they moved forward together with the reserve battalions. Some red SOS rockets went up opposite 6 Brigade but the German line remained quiet. The harassing batteries gradually shortened their range until they were firing on the start line for the creeping barrage and then, at 3.10 am, a flash like a gigantic sheet of lightning ripped from the gun lines, tracers from 111 Vickers Guns drew spider web patterns in the sky and the ground from the barrage line to well beyond the German trenches was quaking and aflame. At Bertangles, Monash 'stopped and, looking for a moment in the direction of the battlefront, his anxiety relieved, turned slowly... and went to his office'. He kept his nerves steady by sketching the head of the French poilu who had chauffeured Hughes two days before.[1]

Captain Lionel Short, whose C Company had carrying duties in 23 Battalion, recalled the tension in the last minutes:

> *Everything was still as death with the intermittent brilliance of the Hun's flares. Every minute or so Moss would say, 'Shortie, what's the time?' I would say 'Ten to three' and so on... The intense subdued excitement seemed to radiate through the air. And at 3.10 am a leaping line of flame burst on the enemy trenches. The scene was enthralling and tremendous. The din was intolerable. You felt a great pity for the men underneath that fire, yet knew it was your salvation.*[2]

The infantry rose from their starting tapes. For Lieutenant Rule in C Company, following behind the leading waves of 4 Brigade on the right of 14 Battalion, the barrage came down,

> *...with the most terrifying crash I've ever heard. Not a bit of use to try and get the men to double, for in the roar of the guns*

3.10 am 4 July 1918. The barrage begins.

and of the shells bursting ahead it was impossible to hear your own shouts. All we could do was to keep going steadily forward, and hope to God that the Hun would be slow in answering his SOS signal, otherwise the chances were we would be cut to ribbons. Just as his SOS – two red lights – went up, two heavy shells fell, one just in front of my platoon, and the other on the right of the company. When we were twenty yards further on, down they came again... a piece from one which burst closest to me hit me in the seat of the pants with an awful wallop... For the next hundred yards I held onto it until I managed to push it into a fold of my trousers where it no longer burnt my flesh.[3]

Commanding Company C of 131 Regiment, which was attached to 42 Battalion, Captain C.M. Gale thought the barrage 'most wonderful'. Forming an almost straight line from the Somme southwards as far as he could see, it was 'laid down so perfectly that we were able to approach it and follow it at about seventy-five yards as ordered, without receiving any casualties from it'.[4]

Others were less fortunate. As most of the 600 guns in action had not been ranged but were firing from map-based calculations only, 'dropshorts', as the infantry sardonically called them, were inevitable and struck several points of the line. At P.8.b.1.1, C Company of 43 Battalion and the attached Americans from Company E of the 131st suffered twenty casualties between them. In a tragic irony, the battalion had deliberately pulled back fifty yards from its start line to avoid this very possibility. Next to them, 15 Battalion opposite Pear Trench lost over twelve dead and thirty wounded to errant rounds. A gun firing short cost Rule six men in the Reserve Wave.

As the smoke screens and the fountains of dust thrown up suffused through the dense fog, an impenetrable murk quickly spread over the battlefield. Shell bursts appeared as dull glows and then disappeared altogether, forcing the infantry to gauge the barrage line from the flashes of air bursting shrapnel. Until they took their lead from the Australians, the keen but inexperienced Americans were especially confused, Company E blundering into the barrage one minute and then losing it the next. Seeing Company A of 132 Regiment caught in the shelling during 13 Battalion's advance, Corporal Michael Roach ran ahead and was killed while waving them back. He rests in Crouy British Cemetery, west of Amiens. Knowing that the tanks moving up could see even less, the infantry also worried about being caught between them and the barrage.

The gloom affected the tanks even more. In the rehearsals, they had caught up with the infantry by four minutes after zero, when the barrage made its first lift, but at 3.14 am most were nowhere to be seen. Trying to find the battalions to which they were attached and avoid running over dead and wounded, they were still groping blindly forward, guided by officers with compasses to ensure they kept some semblance of direction. In many cases the tanks did not reach the infantry until some minutes later.

Pear Trench

Already badly hit by friendly fire on the Start Line, 15 Battalion, with 132 Regiment's Company G attached, experienced the toughest fighting of the battle as a result of the poor visibility. While the remainder pushed past the northern side of Vaire Wood, A Company on the left attacked Pear Trench, which sprawled across P.8.d. Unable because of the short shooting to get closer than 200 yards to the barrage, it fell further behind when the fire lifted. Worse still, shooting from the map combined with no prior observation over Pear Trench meant that the barrage fell either side of it, doing little damage to the position or its garrison.

A Company was barely 200 yards beyond the Start Line and trying to catch the lift when the German machine guns opened up and a line of bombers, looking like wraiths in the mist, suddenly rose from the crops ahead and hurled a shower of stick grenades. Charging the bombers, who withdrew, the Australians stumbled into intact wire

Pear Trench. A machine gun at the apex caused many casualties as the assault came over the high ground on the right. (AWM E02709)

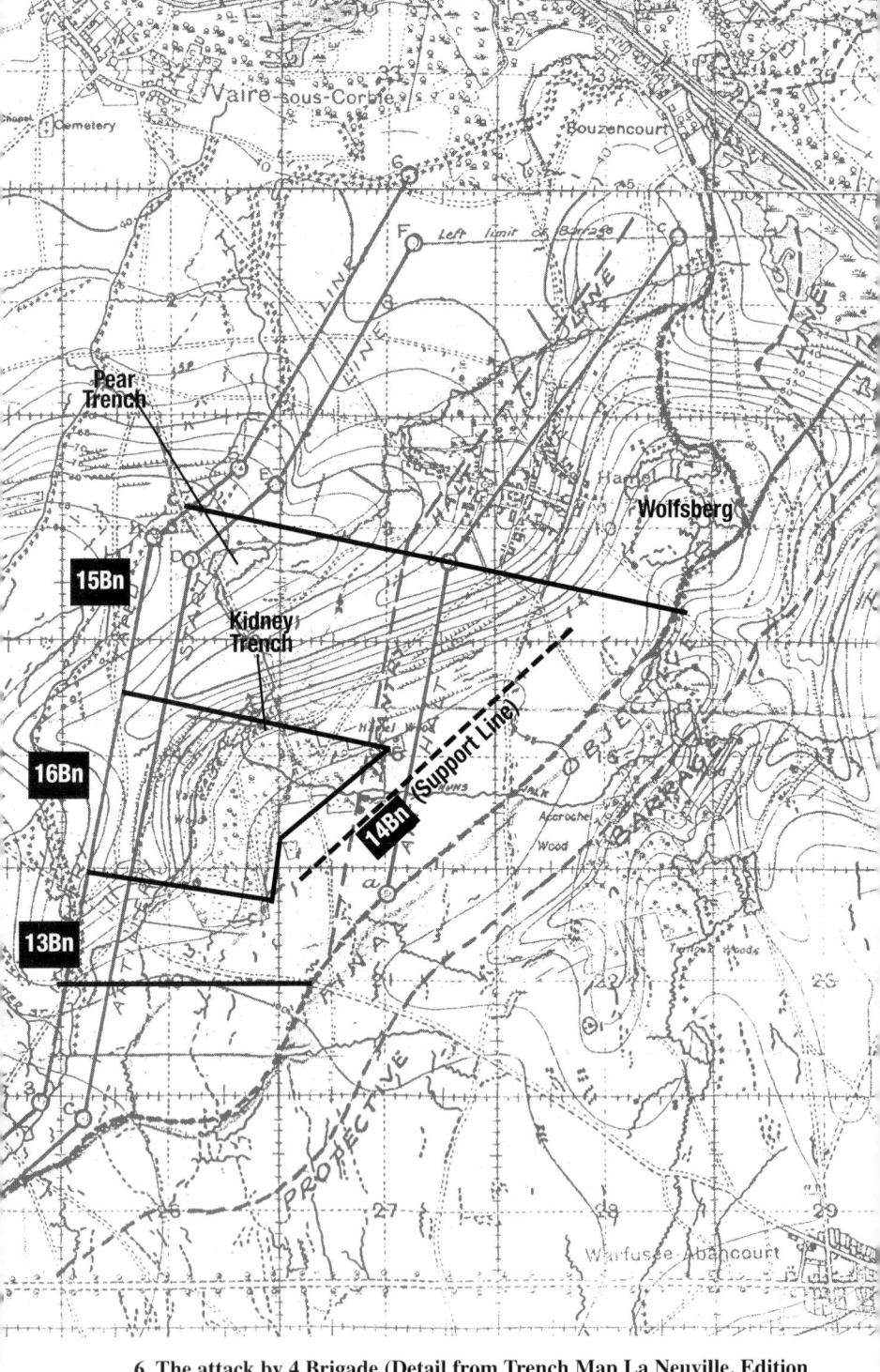

6. The attack by 4 Brigade (Detail from Trench Map La Neuville, Edition 1, 19 June 1918)

entanglements. The front of Pear Trench along the sunken road behind them was also untouched. Fighting their way through the wire but unable to go further, A Company should have lain down and awaited the tanks as instructed. But the three tanks specifically allotted to help it clear the redoubt had lost their way in the murk.

Aware that Pear Trench could enfilade the rest of 15 Battalion between it and the woods and uncertain how long the tanks might be or whether they would arrive at all, A Company assaulted using fire and movement. The two Lewis Gunners in each platoon stood and sprayed from the hip over the crops at the two machine guns holding up the advance. As the riflemen rushed them, a third gun, hitherto silent, began firing. Private Henry Dalziel banged a fresh drum onto the Lewis Gun his mate was firing and leapt, revolver in hand, into the German gun pit. Killing two of the gunners, Dalziel spared the third because, he said, 'The youngster fought so well'. His trigger finger had been shot away but Dalziel twice disregarded orders to seek medical attention. He became the one thousandth recipient of the Victoria Cross. His citation reads:

For most conspicuous bravery and devotion to duty when in action with a Lewis gun section. His company met with determined resistance from a strong-point, which was strongly garrisoned, manned by numerous machine-guns and, undamaged by our artillery fire, was also protected by strong wire entanglements. A heavy concentration of machine-gun fire caused many casualties and held up our advance.

His Lewis gun having come into action and silenced enemy guns in one direction, an enemy gun opened fire from another direction. Private Dalziel dashed at it and with his revolver, killed or captured the entire crew and gun, and allowed our advance to continue. He was severely wounded in the hand, but carried on and took part in the capture of the final objective. He twice went over open ground under heavy enemy artillery and machine gun fire to secure ammunition, and though suffering from considerable loss of blood, he filled magazines and served his gun until severely wounded through the head. His magnificent bravery and devotion to duty was an inspiring example to all his comrades and his dash and unselfish courage at a critical time

Private Henry Dalziel, his head still bandaged, wearing his VC.

German dead on the sunken road at Pear Trench. (AWM E02670)

undoubtedly saved many lives and turned what would have been a serious check into a splendid success.

Though his brain was exposed, Dalziel miraculously survived and returned to Australia in July 1919 after a long convalescence. In 1956 he attended the VC Centenary in London before visiting Hamel and placing a wreath on its cenotaph on 4 July. Aged 72, Dalziel died in Brisbane on 24 July 1965.

In the depth trenches seventy yards behind the sunken road, the Germans held on stubbornly. One machine gunner did not stop firing until he was bayoneted. Other Germans continued to throw grenades, even as those ahead of them surrendered. Infuriated by what they considered to be 'white flag treachery', the Australians moved along the trenches and the sunken road killing any Germans they found. Captain G.H. Mallon from 132 Regiment subsequently counted forty German dead in 'a very small sector'. Moving with his headquarters behind A Company, Lieutenant Colonel T.P McSharry, 15 Battalion's commanding officer and one of the AIF's great fighting leaders, found a number of Germans feigning death in some camouflaged trench mortar pits. When he pelted them with rocks, they realised the game was up and were sent to the rear.

The battalion medical staff set up their Regimental Aid Post in the redoubt, where the stretcher bearers, twelve Australians and four Americans for each company, brought the wounded to be stabilised before taking them to an Advanced Dressing Station one mile in rear. Assisting Major B.C. Kennedy, 15 Battalion's Medical Officer, Lieutenant Frank E. Schramm of the US Army Medical Corps noted the problems that arose with the seriously wounded and the deficiencies in the American medical kits:

> We had some difficulty in getting rid of our dress cases. They were not evacuated fast enough. We had difficulty for a while in obtaining sufficient stretchers. Our supply of Thomas splints [for smashed limbs] ran out and could not be replenished in time. As a consequence we had to use rifles as splints. Of all the cases that I saw and dressed no tourniquet was used. Pressure with the shell dressings was sufficient to check the haemorrhages . . . It was impossible to use diagnosis tags on each case because they came in too fast and to use diagnosis tags would delay the wounded in getting out.
>
> I recommend that our present first-aid packet be replaced by a larger sized dressing, similar to that used by the Australians; that heavy scissors be supplied one to each bearer squad and

Australian and American stretcher bearers clearing the battlefield. (AWM E02691)

Troops from 15 Battalion in a machine gun position in Pear Trench. The superb field of fire is evident. (AWM E02623A)

Machine gun casualties. Australian and American dead before Pear Trench. (AWM E02620)

one to each MO; that an ample supply of Thomas splints, elbow splints and plain board splints be supplied. That cotton or wool be provided in ample quantities and also bandages; that morphine be furnished by the Field Hospital.[5]

Schramm received the Military Cross for his work during the fighting and the US Army Medical Service adopted his recommendations.

The defence of Pear Trench by 55 IR removed the uncertainty that Australian Intelligence had expressed about the fighting value of its parent, the 13th Division. The Westphalians inflicted on 15 Battalion most of its 240 casualties, easily the heaviest of any of the assaulting battalions and close to half its strength. Two hundred yards across and one hundred deep, strongly garrisoned, bristling with well-sited machine guns manned by skilful gunners and with several trench mortars providing extra punch, the redoubt resembled the positions encountered during the offensives on the Somme or Ypres, where unit casualties on this scale were routine. When the tanks did not arrive, the infantry had to advance without any protection from mechanical resources; in other words, to expend itself on heroic physical effort in the old way. It was the very antithesis of Monash's philosophy and the losses were not surprising.

But the run of bad luck that had dogged 15 Battalion now ended. Its northern flank secure, the battalion reached the Artillery Halt Line at the eastern tip of Hamel Wood uneventfully and, in one last irony, the tanks finally found it there. While waiting to move on, its Lewis Gunners shot down two groups of about thirty Germans trying to escape into Hamel village and Accroche Wood.

Vaire and Hamel Woods

As the integrity of a defensive position very much depends on the ability of the localities comprising it to offer mutual support, the battle to capture the position consists of the individual fights to take these localities. Each fight influences those around it and its outcome can determine whether the battle is won or lost. Pear Trench had to fall for 15 Battalion to move past Vaire and Hamel Woods. But its advance also relied on 16 Battalion securing the woods and Kidney Trench, the second redoubt, which enfiladed 15 Battalion's southern flank. In the same way, 16 Battalion needed 15 Battalion to take Pear Trench to anchor its northern flank.

The boundary between 15 and 16 Battalions ran eastwards from P.14.a.5.5, where the Start Line crossed the road that ran almost parallel to the Australian trenches. This point marked the head of a prominent re-entrant that flattened out at Hamel village and whose terraced southern slope rose past Central Copse, which was guarded by a few outposts, to Vaire and Hamel Woods. Partially hidden by Central Copse, Kidney Trench was on the slope below Vaire Wood and one hundred yards west of the sunken road that ran past Pear Trench. It comprised two major trenches and subsidiary posts on a two hundred yard frontage and was sited to enfilade the re-entrant and especially the sunken road. From the redoubt, the German line followed the modern Hamel/Villers-Bretonneux Road, a stretch known as Vaire Trench, to the junction with the Fouilloy-Warfusée Road, today's D122, at P.20.a.5.5.

16 Battalion's six supporting tanks had almost caught up when D Company on the left encountered machine gun fire from the terraced line that ran north from Vaire Wood into Kidney Trench. The Australians attacked through gaps in the wire but it was uncut in front of the redoubt. Just as company headquarters reached the entanglement, a hitherto silent gun opened a devastating fusillade that mortally wounded the company commander, Captain Frederick Woods, and Company Sergeant Major Harold Blinman. The advance faltered. In the neighbouring platoon, Lance Corporal Thomas Axford saw what had happened and charged through one of the gaps, throwing grenades that stunned the machine gunners. He finished them off with his bayonet. A holder of the Military Medal who had been fighting since Pozières in 1916, Axford was awarded the Victoria Cross. His citation reads:

Lance Corporal Thomas Axford VC.

For most conspicuous bravery and initiative during operations. When the barrage lifted and the infantry advanced commenced, his platoon was able to reach the first enemy defences through gaps which had been cut in the wire. The adjoining platoon, being delayed in uncut wire, enemy machine guns got into action, and inflicted many casualties, including the company commander. Lance-Corporal Axford, with great initiative and magnificent courage, at once dashed to the flank, threw his bombs amongst the machine-gun crews, jumped into the trench and charged with his bayonet. Unaided, he killed ten of the enemy and took prisoners; he threw the machine guns over the parapet, and called out to the delayed platoon to come on. He then rejoined his own platoon and fought with it during the remainder of the operations. Prior to the above mentioned, he had assisted in the laying out of the tapes for the jumping off position, which was within 100 yards of the enemy. When the tapes were laid, he remained out in a special patrol to ensure that the enemy did not discover any unusual movement on our side. His initiative and gallantry undoubtedly saved many casualties, and most materially assisted in the complete success of his company in the task assigned to it.

Axford's daring action broke the back of the resistance in Kidney Trench. Deceived by the flavoured smoke fired during the earlier harassing shoots, its garrison was wearing gas masks. Forty-seven prisoners were taken from the dugouts in the sunken road behind the redoubt, many of them very young and small. Woods and Blinman died a few hours later and were buried in a common grave together with Second Lieutenant Horace Blee, who was also gravely wounded in this assault. The three had all been company sergeants major of D Company and were close friends. They rest today in Daours Communal Cemetery Extension, just east of Amiens.

Passing over Vaire Trench, the rest of 16 Battalion entered Vaire Wood. As Companies G and H of 131 Regiment originally attached to it were among those withdrawn, the battalion had to clear the woods alone, its strength halved to 500 men. Although the arrival of its six tanks helped, the trees limited their movement and the smoke from the

The ground across which 16 Battalion assaulted. The barrage has stripped the trees bare. (AWM E03840)

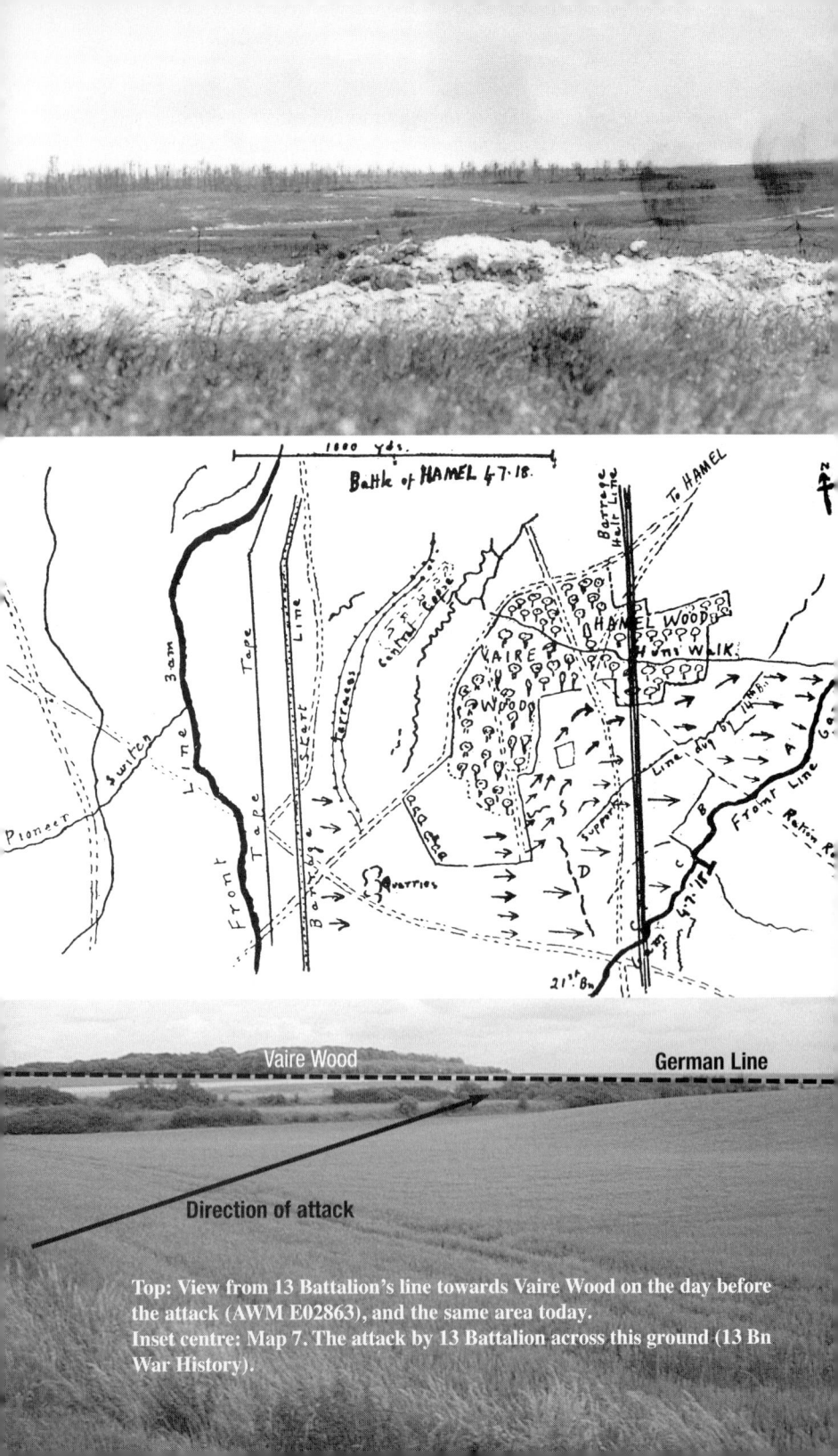

Top: View from 13 Battalion's line towards Vaire Wood on the day before the attack (AWM E02863), and the same area today.
Inset centre: Map 7. The attack by 13 Battalion across this ground (13 Bn War History).

grenades used to signal them was lost in the gloom. The Australians' greatest asset turned out to be the slow pace of the barrage. Stretched out in extended line behind it, they advanced firing from the hip like a posse of western gunfighters and drove the defenders from 13 and 55 IR into the fire, although many escaped along Hun's Walk, the 2,000-yard communication trench that began at Kidney Trench and linked Vaire and Hamel Woods to Accroche Wood.

The line cleared Vaire Wood by 3.50 am and then approached the northeast corner of Hamel Wood, where a German reserve platoon, reinforced by stretcher-bearers and orderlies, made a last stand at their company headquarters. Captain W.J.D. Lynas, DSO, MC summoned a tank at the same time as an Australian lobbed a phosphorous grenade into the main dugout, incinerating several Germans. The remainder surrendered, joining what had been a fairly constant flow of prisoners. According to the 16 Battalion History,

> One party of about a dozen... was led by a German who laughed when one of the diggers said to him, 'Finis le Guerre.' 'Yes, he replied, my ——— oath.' He said he learned the English language on the Boulder mine in Western Australia, and had been called back to the Fatherland early in 1914.[6]

At 4.59 am runners from the Battalion Advance Report Centre, set up where Hun's Walk entered Vaire Wood at P.14.b.6.1, advised that both woods were clear. Having taken 400 prisoners, 16 Battalion began returning to the old Australian line as 4 Brigade's reserve one hour later.

Alongside 16 Battalion meanwhile, 13 Battalion was carrying out the trickiest part of the attack. Stretching 500 yards from P.14.c.2.0 to P.20.a.0.0, its Start Line ran behind the road that parallelled the Australian trenches and through the intersection with the D122 at P.20.a.1.8, 200 yards west of where the German line struck the D122 near a quarry that had been targeted by peaceful penetration in May. The barrage obliterated the post and D Company passed easily 700 yards beyond it to a second quarry at the southern tip of Vaire Wood in P.20.b, where they began digging in after clearing some more posts. Sergeant Victor Lihou, another hip-shooting Lewis Gunner, received the DCM for pouring fire into one while a bombing party crept around the flank to destroy it. From its new position, D Company covered C Company as it pushed 500 yards further to the Blue Line, its right resting on P.21.a.4.0 and its left at P.21.a.9.6.

A and B Companies ran northwards 500 yards to the corner of Hamel Wood and wheeled east to the Blue Line, where they filled the gap between C Company and 15 Battalion, which had moved along the northern side of the wood to P.15.d.9.5 on Hun's Walk. A Company's Captain George Marper, DSO, who had fought as a sergeant at Mouquet Farm, led this rush. When a machine gun engaged his company, he charged it, killing the crew. The eastward swing had just begun with the breaking dawn when two more machine guns opened fire from a concealed trench 200 yards south of the wood and almost on the road that ran through it from Hamel. Many of the trenches in 4 Brigade's area were 'roughly dug and badly undercut [with] apparently no arrangements for sanitation' but this trench was not one of them. It had survived the barrage and was so well camouflaged that aerial reconnaissance missed it.[7]

Badly pinned down, the Australians were saved by the tanks. One of the three supporting 13 Battalion had pressed too close to the barrage and been knocked out but the other two lumbered to within fifty yards of Marper's men. He ran in front of one and was shot twice while pointing out the trench. The tank crushed one of the machine guns, prompting the crew of the second and the other Germans in the position to surrender. While 16 Battalion went on with the clearance of Vaire and Hamel Woods, by 4.18 am A and B Companies were on the Blue Line, linked up with C Company on the right and 15 Battalion on the left. From a starting frontage of just 500 yards, 13 Battalion had fanned out to cover 1,200 yards of the objective, no mean tactical feat. Marper survived.

North and South

In the north, the two front lines diverged sharply. Whereas 11 Brigade's line ran mostly north-south, the German line from Pear Trench headed east for 1,000 yards, made a right-angled turn in front of Hamel and continued in a northeasterly direction for another 1,700 yards before a second abrupt turn carried it due north to the Somme at Bouzencourt. As No Man's Land was at its widest here and the objectives included Hamel and the Wolfsberg, 11 Brigade was given almost half the tank support, twenty-one tanks with six more in reserve.

Strung out on a frontage of 1,000 yards between P.8.b.1.1 and the Cerisy-Hamelet Track, 43 Battalion was to take the village. After being hit by dropshorts, C Company on the right lost the barrage like A Company of 15 Battalion alongside it. While A Company used bayonet and bomb to clear Pear Trench, C Company worked past the northern flank of the position until blocked by a machine gun. Lance Corporal

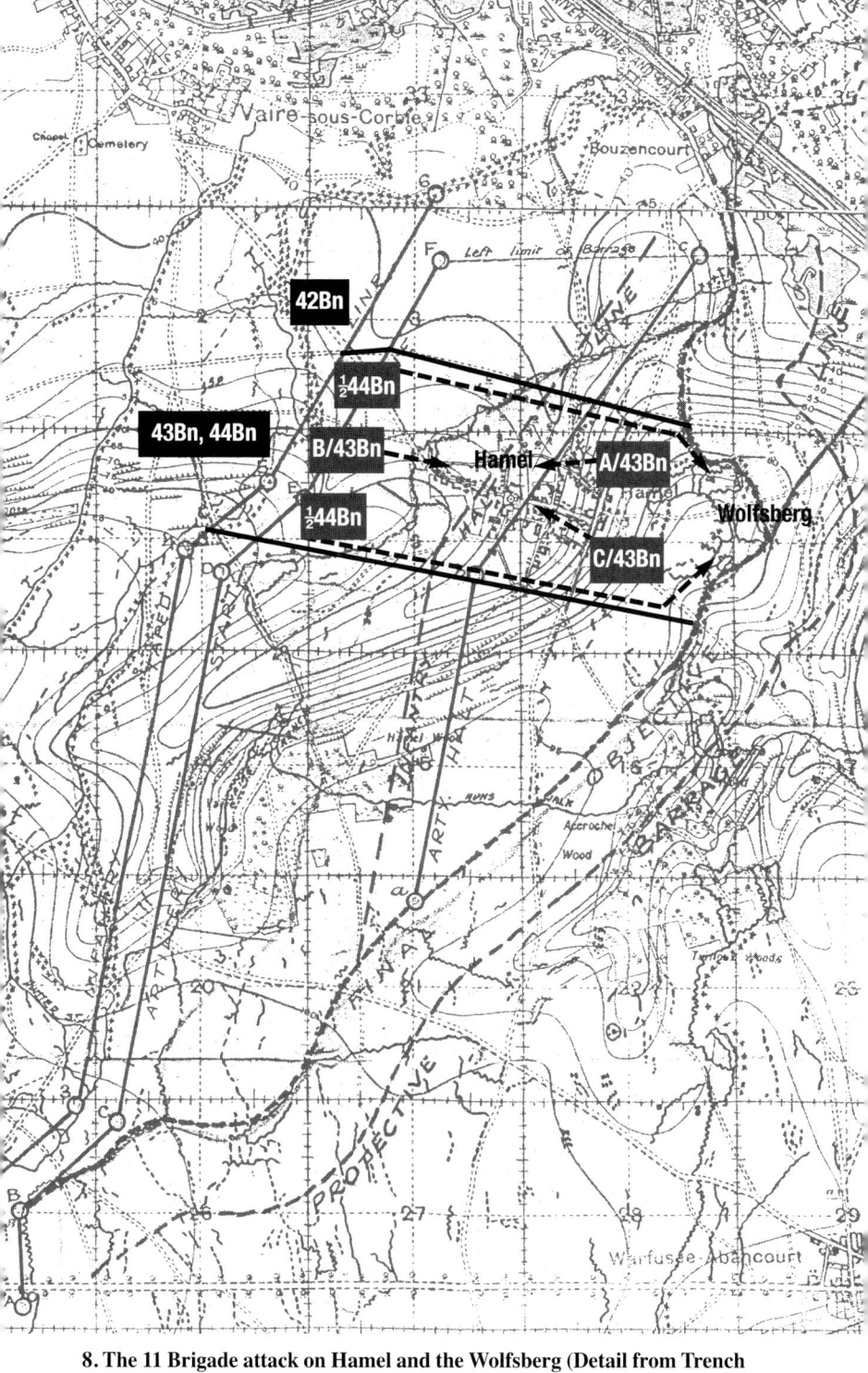

8. The 11 Brigade attack on Hamel and the Wolfsberg (Detail from Trench Map La Neuville, Edition 1, 19 June 1918).

Photo taken after the battle of the area across which 43 Battalion attacked. Notamel Wood fills much of the lower half of the picture and the Wolfsberg is at upper left.

F.M Shaw fired his Lewis Gun from the hip to cover Corporal H.G. Zyburt, an American, while he raced forward to bayonet the three-man gun crew. Wounded, Zyburt received the Military Medal. When the rest of C Company reached the wire further north, they rushed the trench behind it, completely surprising the garrison. Four machine guns were captured with their covers still on.

The remainder of the battalion leant on the barrage for the 800-yard crossing of No Man's Land and met Hamel's defenders, 202 RIR, on the outskirts. By now the shelling had turned the village into an inferno. A flare fired from a dugout behind a big pile of beets at P.9.b.1.7, just south of the road to Vaire at the western tip, illuminated B Company, who in turn could see the Germans, silhouetted against the flames, firing at them. Grenades thrown at the beet pile landed short so Lieutenant I.G. Symons, attached to Company E, led a platoon of the Americans in an outflanking move along the road. When he was in position, the Australians and Americans charged from all sides, killing fifteen Germans and capturing forty from the dugout.

A Company reached Notamel Wood, which extended 450 yards from the northern edge of Hamel to the Cerisy-Hamelet Track, but became disoriented in the dense smoke. Picking out the treetops against the shell bursts, 44 year-old Captain J.T. Moran yelled parade ground orders to get his company back on course. A platoon started bombing northwards along the German line, only to be stopped by a machine gun near the village. Crawling to a tank, the platoon sergeant rang its bell and when the door opened, pointed out the gun to the tank commander. The Germans just managed to flee before their position was flattened. Another tank trundled over to Hamel Wood to crush a troublesome post not yet reached by 15 Battalion. Still another caused consternation to the attackers. Lost in the murk, it waddled back through the advance, dispersing Australians and Americans alike.

Across the Cerisy-Hamelet Track, the width of No Man's Land was a blessing for 42 Battalion, which attacked with A and C Companies on a 700-yard frontage between P.3.b.2.9 and P.3.c.5.7. Blue Cross gas from past German shelling lingered at the northern end of its Start Line near the Somme marshes. A Company forming up there sneezed uncontrollably but the Germans were too far away to hear. Thereafter, the 42nd's advance was trouble free. The German outposts dotting the marshes scattered before it like ducks fleeing a line of beaters. Catching up with the infantry by 3.14 am as planned, the tanks moved back and forth along the barrage crushing likely machine gun posts and fascinating H.S Shapcott:

> It was a weird sight to see these ungainly objects waddling up at the toot, in response to signals from the infantry and approach a machine gun possie with blazing guns. If they did not manage to put the machine gun out of action with their fire they continued straight on and went right over the gun and crew and emplacement and flattened the whole lot out![8]

All battalions of 11 Brigade reached the Artillery Halt Line on time, with 43 Battalion poised to attack Hamel from three sides and 44 Battalion preparing to carry the advance either side of it to the Wolfsberg.

9. The attack by 6 Brigade (Detail from Trench Map La Neuville, Edition 1, 19 June 1918)

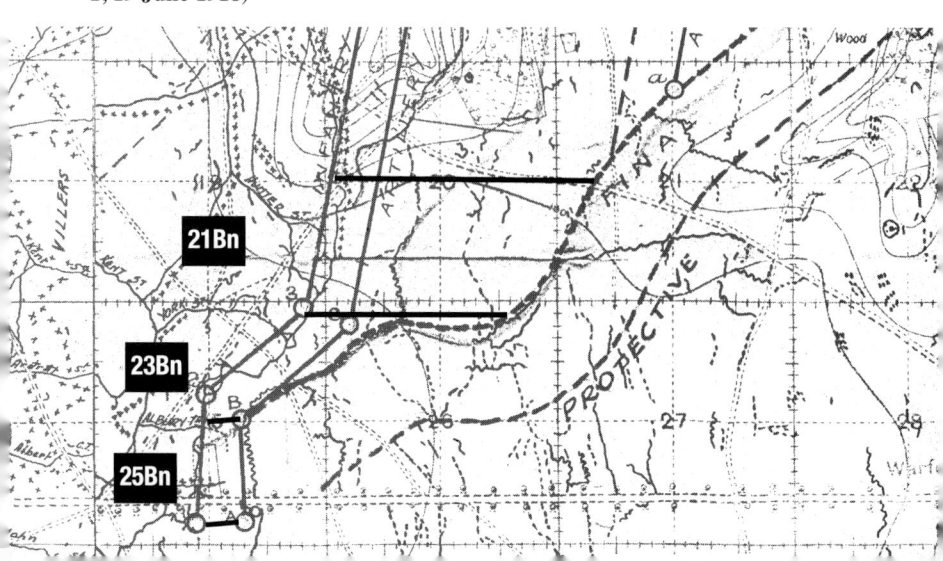

Arcing a mile across the Villers-Bretonneux plateau from P.25.Central to P.21.a.4.0, the Blue Line on the southern flank ended before the Artillery Halt Line began, so 6 Brigade did not have to pause on its way to the final objective. Its advance, which varied in length from 200 yards on the right to over 1,000 yards on the left, came closest to Monash's ideal of mechanical resources helping the infantry forward. The barrage was 'perfect' and the six supporting tanks, shielded by the flank smokescreen, 'had severe fighting and did great execution, their action being of the greatest service', all of which allowed the attack to progress with 'the ease of a field day'.[9] 23 Battalion hugged the barrage so closely that the leading wave was almost punch drunk when it reached 15 IR's trenches. Private Isaac Betteridge was in D Company on the right flank:

> Our own front had a lot of smoke shell that burst in great sheets of fire 30 feet across and looked like golden rain. The old fashioned hell couldn't be as bad and the line of men dropping and lying still, staggering back wounded or lurching drunkenly forward into shellholes, falling over the wire, buffeted by explosions till they looked like devils in their proper environment. Suddenly the enemy trench stood out in front. A line of white cut into the green of the wheat-field. The crowd were firing for moral effect. Some were swearing in a sort of strangled undertone. The reason was to open one's mouth was to get it full of the acid fumes of the explosions. He had not many machine guns. We had the shelter of his trench before he got them going. Into the trench, had to walk over two dead Huns. In a dugout was a poor scared creature that whined and cried like a kiddie that is afraid of the dark. Our officer called on him to come out. The whining continued, to be cut short by a shot. Hope his conscience don't worry him later. The trench we were in was a regular shambles. The sides spattered with blood. Dead men lying everywhere.[10]

D Company eventually ran into stubborn resistance but A and B Companies swept forward effortlessly. Afterwards, the battalion newspaper praised the tanks fulsomely:

> The boys much appreciate the tanks on their Hun-routing excursions. Their ugly appearance and ungainly movement are in themselves sufficient to put the 'wind up', but when their 'for'ard' belches into flame of spitting slaughter, our sympathies should be with the enemy.[11]

On the left, 21 Battalion's three tanks caught up 300 yards from the

Start Line at 15 IR's first trench, whose occupants were wearing gas masks, and crushed it. Only in the third trench did the German machine gunners engage but they were quickly despatched. At 3.59 am, the Battalion Intelligence Officer reported 'Home and dried. Can be seen digging in on Final objective. Tanks are patrolling. Retaliation still slight'.[12] In fact, before the barrage paused for the ten-minute halt, 6 Brigade was on the Blue Line. B and D Companies from 23 Battalion took over a continuous trench in good condition but the rest of the brigade was surrounded by flimsy and scattered bits of trench, some of which had been used as open latrines.

Hamel and Beyond

Dawn had broken when the barrage moved on at 3.51 am, greatly improving visibility. For onlookers in 41 Battalion, held back as 11 Brigade's reserve,

> It was a truly wonderful sight watching the tanks creeping over the ground through the grey mists of dawn, and the long line

Australians from 42 Battalion and attached Americans on the Blue Line (AWM E02690)

of flashing shell-bursts as the barrage lifted and lengthened, while the colossal din of the whole titanic combat smote upon the ears and set the heart palpitating with awe and tense excitement.[13]

When two machine guns stopped 42 Battalion's advance, Lance Corporal M.J. Daley outflanked one and killed the crew with his Lewis Gun and a tank trampled the other. Shortly after 4 am, 42 Battalion arrived on the Blue Line, which followed the northern shoulder of the Wolfsberg down to Bouzencourt between the road and the foot track that lead to the hamlet from today's D71.

Just as A and C Companies from 43 Battalion moved in from the eastern side of Hamel to meet B Company working towards them with the six supporting tanks, hip-shooting Lewis Gunner Lance Corporal Shaw spotted a machine gun two hundred yards away. He charged it, killing a German officer, who rushed at him firing a revolver. When Shaw reached the post, eight Germans lay dead around the gun, whose water-jacket had been punctured by Shaw's fire. As he was about to change magazines, a ninth German attacked him. Drawing his own revolver while they grappled, Shaw smashed the German's skull and then shot him. Three more machine guns opened up. The redoubtable Shaw led an assault on one that captured seventeen prisoners. A tank flattened the other two.

Specially designated sections cleared the cellars and deep dugouts in the village, yielding 300 prisoners from 202 RIR. Conditioned by the flavoured smoke to spend the nights sheltering there, some had their gas masks on and did not realise they were being attacked until the Australians arrived. Indeed, the 43 Battalion War Diary commented that surprise was 'the most outstanding feature' of the attack. 'Everywhere the enemy was unprepared for the assaulting troops. In the front line several M.Gs had their covers still on. Infantry offered only a hurried disorganised resistance and were almost too surprised to surrender.'[14]

Tasked by the Australian Corps Intelligence Chief, Major S.A. Hunn, to look for documents, Lance Corporal B.V. Schulz had noted from air photographs the faint signs of a buried cable that led from Notamel Wood into Hamel. He traced it to a deep dugout and the two German-speaking Americans assigned to him called down to the occupants that grenades would be thrown in if they did not give up and that any treachery afterwards would be dealt with mercilessly. Revolver in hand, Schulz entered the dugout and took the surrender of a battalion commander and his staff of ten. Elsewhere in the village,

Captain Moran ignored the danger of lurking snipers by climbing out on the rafters of a ruined house and raising a French tricolour in order to win a bet.

At 7 am three green flares signalled that Hamel had been cleared and 43 Battalion became 11 Brigade's immediate reserve, A and C Companies occupying positions around the village and B and D Companies returning to the old Australian front line with the prisoners, many of whom were made to carry the Australian wounded. The brigade reserve designated before the fighting, 41 Battalion, took no part and remained in support further back. Half of the tanks were lost. An Australian shell hit one, a German shell another and the third tipped over on the rubble. But the mere approach of a tank was often enough to induce surrender and, in the village as elsewhere, scores of prisoners were dazed and trembling. Indeed, the sight of tanks levelling entire trench lines and rows of shelters left them more shocked than any the Australians had previously seen.

Captain Moran's tricolour flutters above Hamel (AWM E02667)

While 43 Battalion cleared Hamel, 44 Battalion advanced either side of the village, reformed beyond it and started up the bare slope of the Wolfsberg for the Blue Line on the far side of the crest 800 yards eastwards. Seamed with the trenches of the old Amiens Defence Line, which were strongly held by 3/202 RIR and commanded the long, open approaches, the position was effectively another redoubt. No wonder twelve tanks supported 44 Battalion's attack – its own six plus six more to replace those helping 43 Battalion in the village. It needed them. Taking advantage of their excellent fields of fire in the improving light, the German machine guns were in action well before the attack got close.

Australians looking for wounded in Hamel. (AWM EO2666)

As the barrage was mainly shrapnel now, the tanks could move underneath it without risk, which allowed the infantry to hang back more than they normally would. Perfectly placed to deal with the machine guns, the tanks pirouetted over them, to use Monash's term, or fired point blank into the German posts with grapeshot or their own machine guns. The way ahead clear, 44 Battalion rushed the crest, capturing dugouts crowded with men – fifty in one, forty in another and a battalion headquarters in a third. To Bean on the northern heights of the Somme, the Wolfsberg seemed

...like the skyline, so full was the valley of smoke from our smoke shell. Almost immediately after we saw the first tank – and then three or four on either side of it on the skyline behind Hamel and crawling up the hill. Then we could make out a thick line of infantry between the various tanks – at first I thought they were stationary, but they must have been going on to their last objective. [15]

One tank moved backwards and forwards 'like a housewife's flat iron' as it squashed a German post. This tank may have been the same one seen by Private S.L. Huntingdon of 2 Machine Gun Battalion, who likened it to 'some legless insect – perhaps a woodlouse would be the best resemblance', as he witnessed a similar sight to Bean: 'There was another and another to right and left of it and crowds of infantry between them. They were moving towards that skyline along its whole length'.[16]

On 44 Battalion's right, a trench in P.10.d on the southern shoulder of the Wolfsberg heavily engaged 15 Battalion, which summoned a tank officer who was on foot. The firing immediately stopped and some Germans fled when he directed his tank towards it. Hugging the tank as it moved along the trench, the Australians captured twenty-seven light machine guns and took fifty prisoners. Using these machine guns as well as their own, they fired at the Germans escaping down the far slope into the Vallée d'Abancourt, where a number held on in some trenches below the crest. The two battalions linked on the Blue Line at P.10.d.7.3. Further south, the Germans continued to

The ruins of Hamel and (r) the low ground over which 42 Battalion attacked as seen from the Wolfsberg. (AWM E02844B)

The view from above Sailly-le-Sec. Hamel (right centre) is aflame (AWM E02713)

funnel back along Hun's Walk before the inner flanks of 13 and 15 Battalions, advancing either side, sealed it off. Like the defences found by 11 Brigade, the trenches in this area were haphazard, scratchily dug and poorly wired.

Battalions indicated their progress with signal lamps and experimental rockets. But the latter generally landed everywhere except at the headquarters they were supposed to and, in those that were recovered, the message was invariably incinerated. The tanks sent back carrier pigeons. Most reliable of all was the combination of the infantry's matches and flares with No. 3 Squadron. As a 'Strike a Light' patrol flew over the objective sounding its klaxon, pinpricks of red appeared in the trenches and shell holes. They confirmed what some battalions had already transmitted by wireless in one of the first tests of its use so far forward. The Blue Line had been reached along its length and the artillery was firing on the Protective Barrage Line by 4.43 am, ninety-three minutes after the attack started.

In 4 Brigade's area, the manpower shortages in 13 and 15 Battalions resulted in many gaps. As the brigade reserve, 14 Battalion had followed them with defence stores, water and ammunition, which it dumped at the eastern tip of Hamel Wood before digging a support trench 300-500 yards behind the Blue Line. In C Company on the right, Lieutenant Rule's platoon arrived well before the others and came under fire. Seeing Germans lining an earthwork that should have been held by A Company from 13 Battalion, he signalled a tank but it found the trench unoccupied. As it left, a white flag went up and Rule took a party to capture the Germans. The firing resumed. An Australian dropshort and a German bullet killed two of Rule's men, one of them an original member of the Battalion, before the rest reached the trench, which turned out to be Ration Row, a communications sap running southeast towards Accroche Wood.

Following the Germans, who had retreated along it, the Australians came across two dugouts. They were intent on revenge for the 'white flag treachery' but when Rule screamed at the occupants to emerge,

> ...out came two hands with a loaf of black bread in each, and presently a pair of terrified eyes took a glimpse at me... the Huns came out at once, and, when I sized them up, all thoughts of revenge vanished. We could not kill children, and these looked to be barely that. If any of us had been asked how old they were, most of us would have said between fourteen and fifteen, and that was giving them every day of their age. We knew that these babes had not pulled the white flag on us – they were too terrified for that; and, with a boot to help them along, they ran with their hands above their heads back to our lines.[17]

Dressed in an immaculate officer's tunic and riding pants, well-loved eccentric, Lieutenant Ramsay Wood, was sniped through the head alongside Rule while looking for signs of the other Germans. With only three men left, Rule went back to his own line and sent forward two Lewis Guns and some bombers, who cut the Germans off from Accroche Wood. After an hour spent trying to break through, they began to surrender in ones and twos.

One of the Australians' less savoury habits now asserted itself. Captain Gale, who saw the Americans quickly copy their example, commented politely: 'In the taking of German prisoners a tendency was noted on the part of Australian troops to an entire disregard for the

Australian Souvenir King, John Hines with some of his loot.

personal property rights of prisoners of war; they strip them as a rule of anything of personal value'.[18] Though the pun was unintentional, he could have been watching Rule and his men:

> *What a harvest for our boys! Talk about 'ratting'; as each Hun advanced with his hands above his head, several of our lads would dive at him, and, before the astonished Hun knew what was happening, hands were in every pocket, and he was fleeced of everything but his name and his clothes... Near Ramsay Wood's body a new reinforcement was working like a cat on a tin roof, pulling cigars out of a Hun's pocket. In a ferocious manner I asked him if he was not aware of the order that all loot had to be handed to an officer to be sent back to headquarters. He meekly handed them over. I smoked cigars all day, and the rest of the platoon tormented the life out of the youngster for falling to the joke.*[19]

In all, C Company captured fifty-two soldiers from 13 IR and one heavy trench mortar. Lieutenant Wood is buried in Crucifix Corner Cemetery, Villers-Bretonneux.

Next to C Company, A Company had just reached its support position when firing erupted from another gap. Two platoons promptly filled it, capturing twenty-two Germans from 13 IR and three trench mortars, which they turned on Accroche Wood before settling in to enjoy the hot coffee and cigars found in one of the dugouts. Detached to construct a strongpoint, the third platoon assisted D Company from 13 Battalion at the quarry south of Vaire Wood, killing some Germans who refused to leave their dugouts and capturing the rest. Taking more prisoners on the way to the Artillery Halt Line, where it bombed one more dugout, the platoon finally reached the strongpoint site but moved it to cover yet another gap.

Commanded by Lieutenant W. Jacka, brother of the famous VC winner, B Company picked its way through Vaire and Hamel Woods, its right platoon on Huns' Walk. Describing the move forward, the 14 Battalion History graphically remarked on the grisly aftermath of the barrage, which had 'played havoc with the enemy, whose dead bodies could be seen everywhere'.[20] After helping 16 Battalion mop up, B Company sent out a patrol to close a gap and started digging with its right resting on the A Company strongpoint. Except at Pear Trench, where dropshorts killed a Lewis Gun team, D Company on the left had an easy march behind 15 Battalion. It took fifteen prisoners while entrenching on the support line.

Digging In

Daylight heralded a beautiful summer's day. As the Australians occupied the German trenches in many places and the intervening ground offered easy digging, the Blue Line was quickly established. Falling 400 yards east of it, the Protective Barrage continued until 5.13 am, permitting the early release of the tanks. Many stayed on, sometimes with a few Australians or Americans attached, to search the area in between for snipers hiding in the crops.

A few of these teams went through the barrage into Accroche Wood. They did especially good work in front of 15 Battalion, preventing any interference with the consolidation, and in 6 Brigade's area, where fifty Germans surrendered to a tank after the infantry pointed out their post. Another tank waded into a trench complex astride the Roman Road 1,500 yards beyond the new Australian line and was still lumbering about at 5.30 am when the rest had left for their rallying points five miles rearward, taking wounded infantry with them. Of the sixty fighting tanks that left the Jumping Off Line, only three broke down and the Germans knocked out just one of the five that were disabled. All five were salvaged within forty-eight hours. Thirteen tank crewmen were wounded, five of them slightly. No Australian or American wounded were run over.

Though the fighting tanks had carried ammunition and water for the

Exhausted troops from 15 Battalion asleep in a German trench mortar pit. It is solidly built and camouflaged.

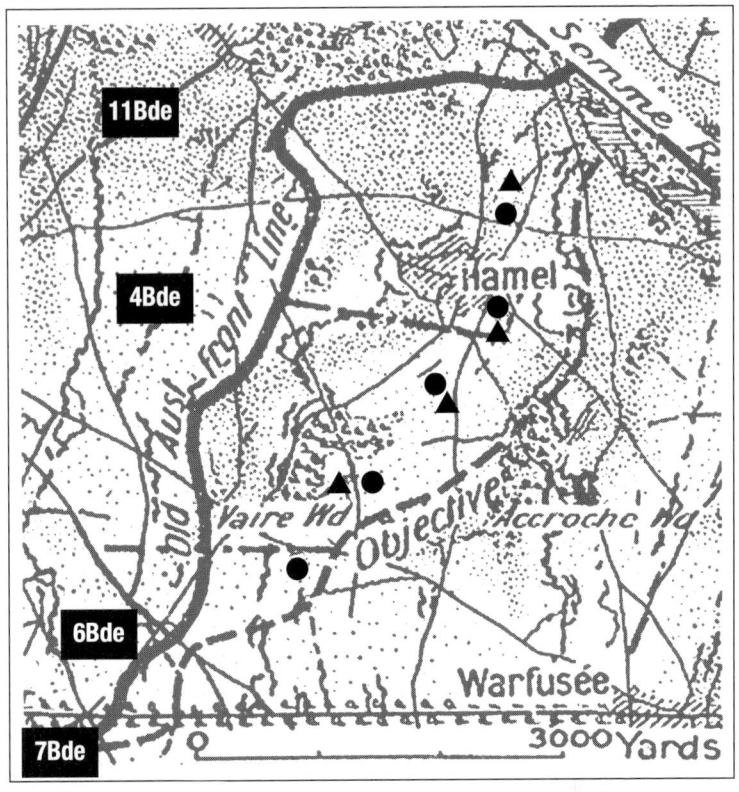

10. Ammunition drop zone ● and carrier tank dumping point ▲ locations.

infantry, the four carrier tanks were the unsung heroes of the consolidation. Each one delivered a 12,500lb load to prearranged dumps 400 yards from the Blue Line within half an hour of the infantry arriving. 11 Brigade relied on them almost exclusively but 4 Brigade's use of 14 Battalion for many of its needs suggests a scepticism that probably explains why Lieutenant Colonel Marks was stunned by what he saw in 13 Battalion's dump after the carrier tank had left: 134 coils of barbed wire, 450 screw pickets, 45 sheets of corrugated iron, 50 tins of water, 150 trench mortar bombs, 10,000 rounds of ammunition and 20 boxes of grenades. If each man carried 40lbs, then 1,250 men would have been needed to cart what the carrier tanks brought forward. One infantry commander thought that the outstanding lesson of the battle lay in this achievement.[21]

No. 9 Squadron dropped 112,000 rounds of ammunition. This time the reports were 'favourable but not enthusiastic'. As the method was largely untried, most of the ninety-three boxes fell some distance from the drop zones and the target markers and the Germans recovered two that drifted into Accroche Wood. One aircraft supporting 11 Brigade was either hit by an artillery shell or, more likely, structurally damaged when a parachute became entangled around its wings. The photograph of its final plummet is one of the most dramatic of the war. Another ammunition carrier was lost when thirty German aircraft showed up

An R.E.8 makes its final plummet during the battle. (AWM E03912)

Australians examining the wreckage. (AWM E03844)

just after the British fighter cover withdrew at 9.30 am. No. 3 Squadron managed to shoot down two while flying its observation patrols.[22]

German aerial observers began directing their surviving guns, turning what had hitherto been a feeble response into a heavy concentration on Hamel and the Wolfsberg. Despite the shelling, a party from 43 Battalion under Corporal T. Ryan recovered 73,000 rounds of ammunition and several cases of grenades from a burning house in the village, the contents of a British dump abandoned during the March retreat. With the tanks gone, the problem everywhere else was sniping, which became so severe on the right flank that 6 Brigade suspended wiring until its own snipers came up. But by 10.30 am the Blue Line was everywhere wired in and the support trenches behind it completed. Violating the Geneva Convention, 11 Brigade had press-ganged its prisoners into helping.

At 11 am and again at noon, the artillery scattered about eighty Germans in the Vallée d'Abancourt. Australians and Americans continued to roam No Man's Land. Corporal Alexander Hutchison from 23 Battalion captured two machine guns and killed fifteen Germans as they fled, winning the DCM. Corporal Fred Miller and Private James O'Meara from the same unit took thirteen prisoners and a machine gun when they seized a trench 200 yards from the Blue Line. A patrol from 15 Battalion killed several Germans and captured five prisoners and four machine guns from a post it rushed at 2 pm. 5 Brigade's aircraft dropped 1,100 25 lb bombs and 58 112 lb bombs during the day. Amazed at how smoothly the attack had gone, experienced Australians speculated out loud; 'There's a catch in this somewhere – it's too easy'.[23] They were right to wonder.

Counterattack on the Wolfsberg

At nightfall, 44 Battalion prepared to clear the strongpoint below the crest of the Wolfsberg, in which the remnants of the garrison were still holding out. The Germans got in first. At 10 pm a heavy bombardment fell and 300 men from 1/202 RIR, the 43rd Division's reserve south of the Somme, swarmed up the communication trench from the strongpoint behind a line of bombers and quickly captured a 200-yard stretch of the Blue Line around P.11.a.1.7. A powerful fifteen minute barrage crashed down on the German rear following the firing of the SOS signal at 10.10 pm and 11 Brigade's Stokes mortar battery, awash with bombs from the carrier tanks, pounded the communication trench, greatly impeding the passage of reinforcements and supplies.

The companies either side of the breach planned to close it by attacking inwards but had used up the Battalion's stock of grenades to contain the Germans. A Company from 43 Battalion left Hamel with more, accompanied by two bombing sections and some Americans as reinforcements for 44 Battalion. During the wait, the Australian artillery fired four more bombardments and the Germans guns kept up a steady rain of phosgene and mustard gas, all of which deepened the confusion that is inseparable from a night engagement. Co-ordinated by runners who skirted around the fighting, the double assault did not get underway until 2 am. The Germans were waiting. Well-established behind trench blocks, they stopped the southern drive of Captain W.J. Stables' company with showers of grenades.

Bombing northwards, parties under Lieutenants F.O. Gaze and C.R. Cornish made better progress, thanks largely to the heroics of Private James Lynch, a giant who had been an axeman before the war. Throwing grenades and wielding a club, he drove the Germans from bay to bay and back down the communication trench until shot through the head. Just then the Germans broke and the Australians tore after them across the open ground, hurling grenades and spraying Lewis Guns from the hip. Yelling 'I see it!' when a machine gun opened up, Corporal Thomas Pope, one of the Americans from 43 Battalion, charged, bayoneting the crew and shooting nearby Germans with his

Stretcher-bearers resting on the Cerisy-Hamelet track, along which wounded and prisoners were evacuated to a backloading point in Hamelet. Hamel is centre picture. (AWM EO2701)

rifle. Pope won the US Army's first Medal of Honor in France and the British DCM. The two citations are interesting because they describe the same action but disagree on the time and place. Pope's Medal of Honor citation reads:

> His company was advancing behind the tanks when it was halted by hostile machinegun fire. Going forward alone, he rushed a machinegun nest, killed several of the crew with his bayonet, and, standing astride this gun, held off the others until reinforcements arrived and captured them.

The DCM citation, however, is far more specific, and almost certainly refers to the action on the Wolfsberg:

> At Hamel, on the evening of 4th July 1918, the enemy having captured one of our advanced posts by counter attacks, the first platoon of E Company was ordered to restore the position. Corporal Pope rushed a hostile machine-gun single-handed, bayoneted several of the crew and standing astride of the gun kept the remainder of the detachment at bay until the arrival of reinforcements and the gun-crew were all killed or captured.

The rush continued until the strongpoint from which 1/202 launched its counterattack was captured. Fifty prisoners, including six officers, and ten machine guns were taken from the dugouts the Germans briefly occupied on the Blue Line. Eleven Australians held in a dugout used as an aid post were freed and commented on their kindly treatment, one having had his wounds dressed by a German medic. Four others, stretcher-bearers the Germans sent back with one of their own wounded, remained captive. The artillery harassed the German line throughout the night and supported 13 Battalion when it erased a post on the right flank in a final flurry at 3 am on 5 July.

The Diversions

According to the Australian Corps' preliminary report on the battle, the 5th Division's diversionary operations between the Somme and the Ancre convinced the Germans that the main blow was being delivered there.[24] They responded with a very heavy barrage fifty-three minutes after zero hour, which helped keep the real attack south of the Somme relatively free of artillery interference. From 55 Battalion's trenches above Sailly-Laurette at K.25.c.5.7, Lieutenant W.E. Campbell and five of his men waved fifteen papier-maché dummies in Australian uniforms with slung rifles, giving the impression that over one hundred men had gone over the top. Continued until 3.45 am, the 'Chinese' attack drew torrential machine gun fire that riddled the figures. They

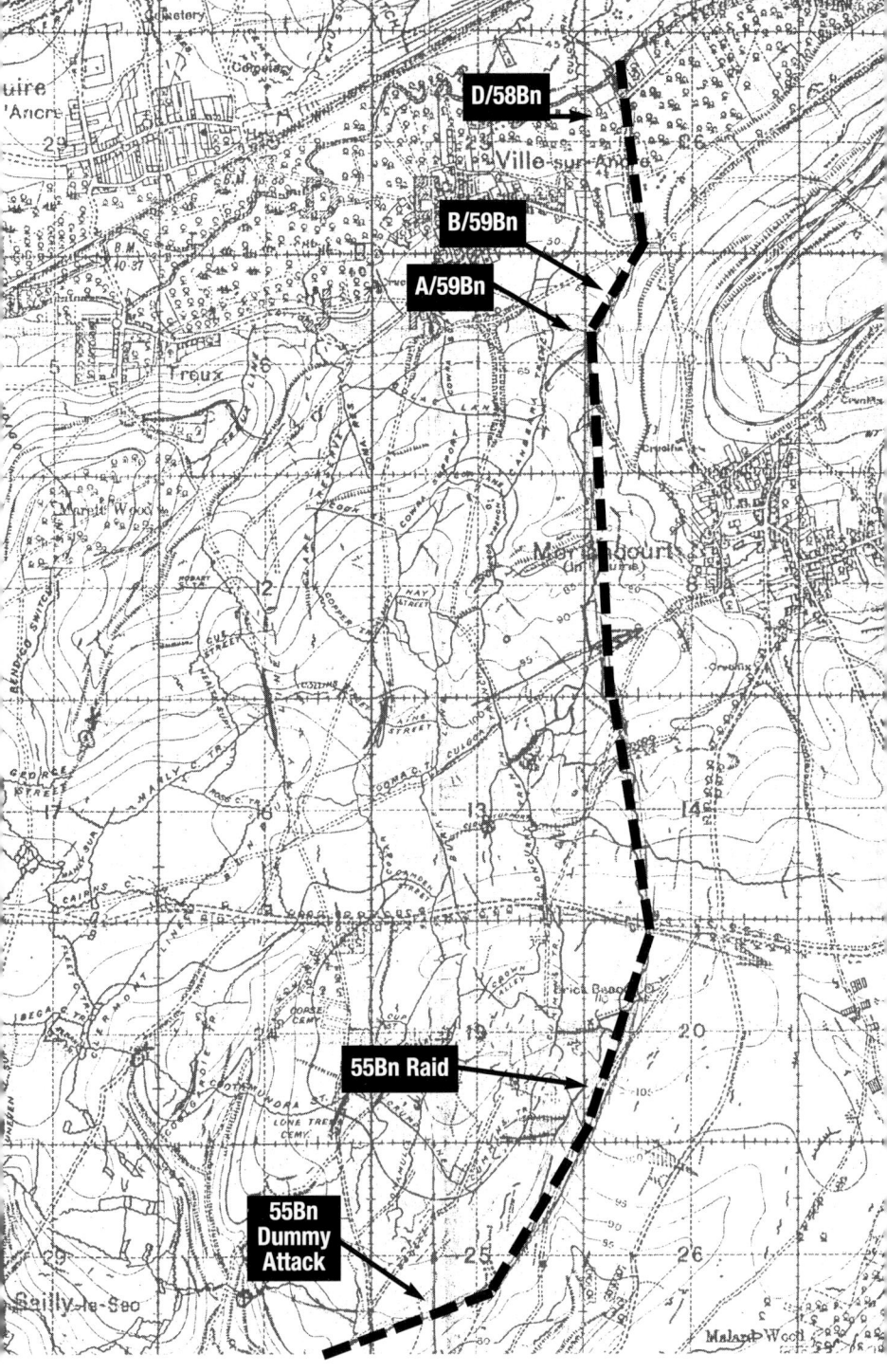

11. The diversions north of the Somme.

12. 55 Battalion's raid near the Brick Beacon (based on map in 55 Battalion War Diary).

were the only casualties.

Conversely, the raid on the two German trenches in K.19.d and K.20.c near the Brick Beacon cost 55 Battalion heavily. The Germans answered the barrage with a heavy trench mortar pounding of the area where Captain K.R. Wyllie and the 200 raiders were lying on the starting tape waiting for their own artillery to advance. Unable to go forwards or backwards, the Australians lost seven men killed and twenty-nine wounded before the barrage lifted and several more to machine gun fire when they rushed the first German line one hundred yards away. Those in it were killed apart from one taken prisoner.

The second wave raced through the flimsy belt of wire protecting the next line. They destroyed several dugouts but could take only two more prisoners and two machine guns as the Germans fought back strongly. Struggling to keep direction in the dense smoke, Wyllie's men had to withdraw through the German SOS barrage, which began nine minutes after zero. All told, they suffered sixty-seven casualties. The Germans, from 232 RIR of the 107th Division, lost only ten. Their trenches were 'very well dug, 6' deep and firestepped'.[25]

From the line captured east of Ville in May, 15 Brigade launched the biggest of the 5th Division's feints, attacking astride the Ville-Méaulte Road, the modern D120, on a frontage of 1,200 yards to seize the 107th Division's positions 500 yards away across the Vallée de Ville between K.1.b.9.2. and the Ancre. Brigadier General Elliott had urged the operation on his divisional commander, Major General Hobbs, as a night assault because he wanted the new line thoroughly consolidated by daylight, when shelling from the Morlancourt Heights overlooking it would be heavy. He was furious when Hobbs offered it as a diversion for the Hamel attack because his men would have to dig in after dawn in full view of the Germans.

North of the D120, where the Ancre flats were a morass of marshy woods, 52 RIR on the 107th Division's right flank held a few scattered posts along the only dry ground, a 750-yard stretch of road that left the D120 for the river and headed northeastwards across it to Dernancourt. Creating an AIF record for a company frontage, the eighty men of D Company 58 Battalion, under Captain Forbes Dawson, attacked this line. Though they had rehearsed daily, the assault started badly when the commander of a reserve platoon, sent forward to support Dawson's left, blundered past an Australian listening post and was badly wounded by a grenade. But the barrage was very accurate, Dawson yelling, 'Come on boys, they're off', as it lifted. He was instantly wounded but kept going behind his three widely separated platoons.

13. 15 Brigade's attack at Ville-sur-Ancre.

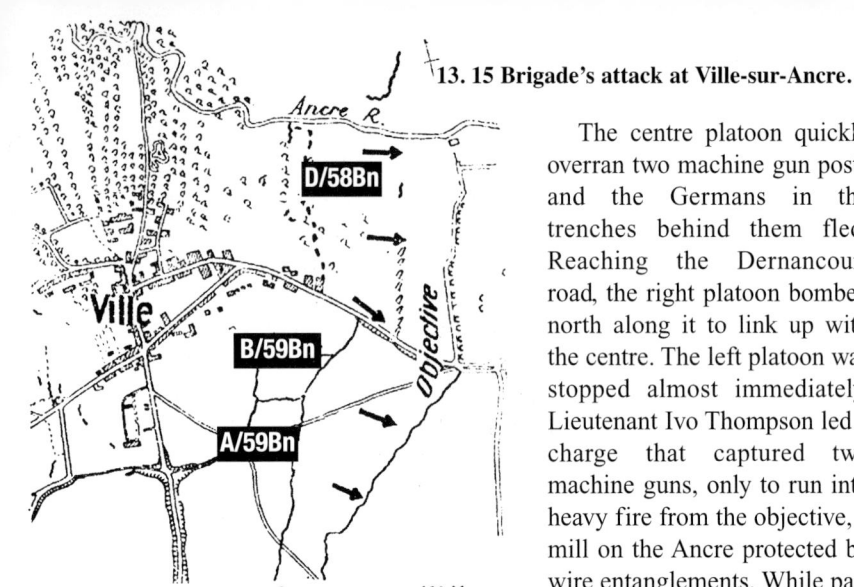

The centre platoon quickly overran two machine gun posts and the Germans in the trenches behind them fled. Reaching the Dernancourt road, the right platoon bombed north along it to link up with the centre. The left platoon was stopped almost immediately. Lieutenant Ivo Thompson led a charge that captured two machine guns, only to run into heavy fire from the objective, a mill on the Ancre protected by wire entanglements. While part of his platoon attacked frontally, Thompson led another charge from the flank that took the mill along with three more machine guns. A fourth killed him. As the casualties were heavy, Dawson sent the reserve platoon to reinforce the position, while a platoon from 57 Battalion extended the line to the centre platoon 300 yards south. Thompson rests in Ribemont Communal Cemetery Extension, southwest of Albert.

Two companies from 59 Battalion attacked from Canberra Trench south of the D120, where 52 RIR held a continuous line on the drier ground. When Captain G.W. Akeroyd's A Company on the right charged, the Germans fled and Second Lieutenant Stephen Facey, though wounded, barricaded their trench. The right platoon of Captain K.G. McDonald's B Company knocked out a machine gun on the way over but three more caught the centre in wire concealed by the crops. Half of these men became casualties and McDonald ordered the survivors to make their way to the right platoon. As the left platoon had also reached the trench, bombers were able to work inwards from both ends to clear it. McDonald's Lewis gunners shot down a counterattack.

After another counterattack at the other end of the line wounded Akeroyd and killed Facey, Sergeant P.L. Little, DCM, MM, a barber in civilian life, took charge, withdrawing the six men who were left fifty yards past the barricades, where they waited while grenades were brought up. When they arrived, Little led an attack that bombed the Germans well beyond the barricades, whose rebuilding he then supervised. Whenever the Germans fired flares for their artillery, the Australians sent up contradictory ones to confuse them.

15 Brigade had taken its entire objective, capturing fifteen machine guns and inflicting at least 140 casualties on 52 RIR. Elliott ordered a company from 60 Battalion to reinforce the new line but the Germans did nothing until 8.50 pm, when they began shelling it. Seeing their infantry forming up on the Morlancourt Heights, McDonald called down an SOS barrage, which continued for eighty minutes. Along with the counterattack preparations, the German fire ceased. But it killed one of 15 Brigade's outstanding officers, Lieutenant John Moore, who had won the Military Medal as a private soldier and the Military Cross twice after he was commissioned. He is buried in Méricourt-l'Abbé Communal Cemetery Extension, on the D120 two miles west of Ville. Facey, who won the DCM as a sergeant, also rests there.

On the extreme right, Brigadier General Wisdom had rejected a diversionary raid by 7 Brigade in favour of taking advantage of the main attack by seizing 137 IR's line opposite 25 Battalion. As this operation was subsidiary and involved a maximum advance of 200 yards astride the Roman Road, no tanks were allotted. Still, a barrage from nineteen machine guns covered it and the Australian Heavy Trench Mortar Battery reinforced the artillery barrage by lobbing its massive 9.45-inch bombs onto the 108th Division's positions in Monument Wood and along the railway line. Nonetheless, 137 IR resisted fiercely well after the two attacking companies of 25 Battalion reached the German trenches and the fighting spilled across P.25.b.3.0, through which its boundary with 23 Battalion ran. D Company on the left had a brief but savage bayonet fight before securing its line at 3.35 am.

South of the Roman Road, the post at P.25.d.3.3, which was on 25 Battalion's right flank, put up such a stiff fight that Sergeant C.G. Ham and eight others were the only men from the two assaulting platoons of B Company who survived to make the final rush that took it. Moving along the road and up the trench from the south, 3/137 IR counterattacked them at 4.20 am. Ham fired the SOS signal, bringing down an artillery and machine gun barrage, but enough Germans got through to threaten the position. A platoon from D Company arrived in the nick of time, whereupon German morale 'completely gave way', Major H.H. Page, the battalion commander, reported, 'and parties of twos and threes, and in one case ten, came in and surrendered from distances up to 350 yards from our objective'. Wisdom thought them the poorest lot of prisoners he had ever seen but 3/137 IR's old line was found to be in excellent condition.[26]

The Other Side of the Hill

From the German standpoint the tanks and artillery made the attack hard to resist, but the absence of any warning wrongfooted them completely. Some wondered at the non-stop air operations but nobody guessed that tank noise was being masked. An officer captured by 4 Brigade stated that he heard movement in the crops but dismissed it as a wiring party. When the noise continued, he thought a raid was being prepared and stood his men to. The SOS flares seen by 6 Brigade during the harassing fire were the only outward sign of German concern. All along their line, the scale of the attack and the means employed took the Germans by surprise and many, especially in Hamel, were caught in their dugouts by the sheer speed of the assault. The barrage destroyed most of the forward communications and the smoke and mist prevented observation, further reducing the chance of a co-ordinated response.

Consequently, the headquarters in rear did not know what had happened. On the southern flank, the 108th Division remained in blissful ignorance for so long that the German High Command used it as an example of poor command and control. Surviving records from the 43rd Reserve Division indicate that 202 RIR's headquarters did not find out that the two forward battalions around Hamel had been overrun until the following picture emerged at 5.45 am:

> In the sector south of the Somme several tanks broke through followed by infantry. Some tanks proceeded past Hamel to the Wolfsberg; others turned and mopped up the German trenches. The fighting in Hamel lasted $1-1\frac{1}{2}$ hours and during that time heavy fighting was going on on the Wolfsberg. The tanks and the following infantry were attacked by the troops (incl. M.G. nests) in immediate support but the fire of the M.Gs. was much impaired by the thick smoke which lay on the Berg. The enemy succeeded in gaining the most southern trenches on the Wolfsberg and then possession of the whole western trench; the trench to the east was held in spite of repeated attacks.[27]

In the 13th Division, 55 IR's headquarters was alerted at 5.20 am, that of 15 IR at 7.20 am and the headquarters of 13 IR even later. Only twenty-one men and the headquarters of 2/15 IR, half a mile beyond the Blue Line, survived the attack. The battalion commander, Cavalry Captain Freiherr von Preusschen, described the fate of the rest:

> First, at 3 am, came drumfire. Only a quarter of an hour later headquarters heard in the direction of the front strong infantry fire. Soon after tanks appeared on the Roman Road (1,000 yards

to the south) and the area north of it. Tanks went beyond battalion headquarters and then turned. When, at 5 am, English infantry was visible ahead, battalion headquarters knew that its companies had been overrun'.[28]

Preusschen pulled his headquarters back at 5 pm, not without difficulty, as the Australians were probing around it.

The slow passage of information nullified the important defensive principle of having reserves ready to counterattack before the ground lost can be consolidated. Digging in on the Blue Line was well underway when first news of the attack finally reached the 43rd Reserve Division. It ordered 1/202 RIR, the reserve battalion south of the Somme at Méricourt, and 1/201 RIR north of the river to the Vallée d'Abancourt. The move was very much delayed by bombing and strafing from 'enemy aircraft flying at 30 metres' so that 1/202 RIR and 1/201 RIR did not reach the area until 8.20 am and 10.45 am respectively. Aware by then that the Wolfsberg had been lost, the divisional headquarters ordered 1/202 RIR to retake the feature by counterattacking through the remnants of 3/202 IR under Lieutenant Paulsen on the eastern edge. But its assembly was detected by 44 Battalion and heavily shelled, further delaying the counterattack until 10 pm.

According to the German record, the three companies of 1/202 IR 'succeeded after heavy fighting in clearing the majority of trenches on the Wolfsberg of the enemy, taking thereby six prisoners of the 3rd Aust Div and 4 M.Gs'. At this point, when its own casualties and increasing resistance from 44 Battalion halted 1/202 IR, 1/201 IR should have been thrown in. Perhaps because of confusion or poor communications, it was not sent forward until 2.30 am on 5 July. As 44 Battalion's counterattack had swept 1/202 IR off the crest before it arrived, 1/201 RIR played no part in the fight and withdrew eastwards. Asked for an explanation by the commander of XI Corps, who was contemplating an inquiry, the 43rd Reserve Division's commander attributed the loss of Hamel to:

Lack of a good defensive system – the old French trenches were unsuitable for defence against the west. Unfinished state of the main line of resistance on the Wolfsberg owing to insufficient labour. Absence of any lightly held forward zone, which made the penetration of tanks easier. The thick smoke caused by enemy artillery preparation. The continuous attacks from the air which had weakened the reserves before they were employed; had the reserves come in earlier and in full strength, the Wolfsberg might have been completely recaptured. No report of tanks being observed or heard before the battle.

The Division considered that the troops could not be blamed and that there was no occasion for any enquiry to be held with the thought of fixing culpability on any particular person.[29]

The Germans had also planned a counterattack against 15 Brigade on the Ancre, lending 247 RIR from the 54th Reserve Division, which had been held at Dernancourt, to the 107th Division for the task as 52 RIR's chances were recognised as slim. But the preparatory shelling attracted much stronger retaliation, scattering 247 IR's assembly on the Morlancourt Heights and forcing the abandonment of the counterattack. 52 RIR was left sorting out its disorganised companies to hold the old support trenches as the new front line.

NOTES

1. Coxen to *Reveille; War Letters*, pp. 249-50.
2. Short cited in R. Austin, *Forward Undeterred. The History of the 23rd Battalion 1915-1918* (Slouch Hat Publications, 1998), p. 166.
3. Rule, op. cit., p. 302-3.
4. Gale cited in *OH. VI*, pp. 284-5.
5. Schramm cited in Laffin, *Hamel*, pp. 109-110.
6. C. Longmore, *The Old Sixteenth* (16 Battalion Association, 1929), p. 183; see also Appendix 2 to 16 Battalion War D, July 1918, Item 23/33, Roll 4, AWM 4.
7. 'Notes on Hamel Offensive', 12 July 1918, Appendix 96 to 4 Brigade War D, July 1918, Item 23/4, Roll 9, AWM 4.
8. Shapcott, *War Babies*, p. 194.
9. OH. VI, p. 297; 5 Tank Brigade After Action Report (G.50/6), 13 July 1918, Item 358/17, AWM 26.
10. Betteridge cited in *Forward Undeterred*, pp. 168-9.
11. Cited in *Forward Undeterred*, p. 167.
12. Entry for 4 July 1918, 21 Battalion War D, Item 23/38, Roll 54, AWM 4. See also 'Preliminary Report on Operations of 6th A.I. Brigade on 4-7-1918', Appendix X to 6 Brigade War D, July 1918, Item 23/6, Roll 13, AWM 4.
13. *The Forty-First 1914-1918*, undated, p. 106.
14. Entry for 4 July 1918, 43 Battalion War D, Item 23/60, Roll 79, AWM 4.
15. Bean, D116, 4 July 1918.
16. *OH. VI*, p. 307; Huntingon to Hilda, 20 September 1918, PR00654, AWM.
17. Rule, op. cit., p.305.
18. Gale cited in *OH. VI*, p. 333.
19. Rule, op. cit., p. 306.
20. N. Wanliss, *The History of the Fourteenth Battalion AIF* (Arrow, 1929), p. 307.
21. 'Capture of Hamel and Hamel Ridge'; 5 Tank Brigade After Action Report; OH. VI, p. 305.
22. F.M. Cutlack, *OH. The Australian Flying Corps* (Angus & Robertson, 1923), p. 274.
23. *OH. VI*, p. 311.
24. 'Capture of Hamel and Hamel Ridge'.
25. 'Report on 55 Battalion Minor Operation on 4 July 1918', Appendix 8 to 55 Battalion War D, July 1918, Item 23/72, Roll 92, AWM 4.
26. 'Report on the Operations of July 4th 1918', Appendix B to 25 Battalion War D, July 1918, Item 23/42, Roll 59, AWM 4; R. Donelley, *Black Over Blue. The 25th Battalion AIF at War 1915-18,* (USQ Press, 1997), pp. 132-3.
27. 'German Records Relative to Australian Operations on the Western Front', compiled by Captain J.J. Herbertson (Class No. 111.050), AWM.
28. Quoted in *OH. VI*, p. 314.
29. 'German Records Relative to Australian Operations on the Western Front'.

Chapter Five

AFTERMATH

The battle cost the Australians about 1,200 casualties. In the main attack, 4, 6 and 11 Brigades suffered 504, 131 and 312 casualties respectively, while 7 and 15 Brigades lost 115 and 142 men in the flank diversions. The Americans had 176 casualties. German losses were much heavier, amounting to over 2,000 men, 177 machine guns, two field guns, thirty-two trench mortars and three anti-tank rifles. Over 1,600 prisoners were taken. Most of the front line battalions from 52 and 202 RIR and 13, 15, 55 and 137 IR had to be reduced temporarily to a single company. The outcome represented the BEF's first major offensive success since the opening day at Cambrai eight months earlier. No battle within his previous experience, wrote Monash, 'not even Messines, passed off so smoothly, so exactly to timetable, or was

German prisoners assembled near 4 Brigade battle headquarters, Hamelet. (AWM E02698)

Generals Monash (right) and Sinclair-MacLagan accompany M. Clemenceau during his visit to Australian troops after the battle. (AWM E02527)

so free from any kind of hitch'.[1]

At the Supreme War Council, which was in session at Versailles when news of the victory arrived, Lloyd George and the Prime Ministers of Canada, New Zealand and Newfoundland asked Hughes to cable their congratulations to Monash. The French Prime Minister, Georges Clemenceau, decided to visit the Australians instead of making his weekly call on a French division. Dressed in his customary brown suit and crumpled felt hat, he arrived at the 4th Division's headquarters at Bussy-les-Daours on Sunday 7 July. Gasping for breath through emotion and asthma, Clemenceau enthralled the Hamel veterans gathered in a circle around him with an address in English that entered Australian folklore:

> *When the Australians came to France, the French people expected a great deal from you because they had heard what you*

have accomplished in the development of your own country. We knew that you would fight a real fight, but we did not know that from the very beginning you would astonish the whole continent. I shall go back tomorrow and say to my countrymen: 'I have seen the Australians. I have looked in their faces. I know that these men will fight alongside of us again until the cause for which we are all fighting is safe for us and for our children'.

Sinclair-MacLagan led three cheers for France and Clemenceau remarked 'De jolis enfants', as he left. Haig was delighted with this 'nice success' that secured the Villers-Bretonneux plateau. The odd man out was Pershing. Peeved at the participation of the four companies from the 33rd Division despite his instructions to the contrary, he reiterated to Haig in instructions 'so positive that nothing of the kind could occur again', that all plans to use American troops attached to the BEF for training must be referred to him personally.[2]

After the war, Monash made exaggerated claims for the battle. Far from originating in a desire to allay the 'anxiety and nervousness of the public' or to get commanders to 'think offensively', it was launched for local tactical reasons. As for an 'electric effect' that 'stimulated many men to the realisation that the enemy was not invulnerable', General Mangin had probably never heard of Monash when the French Tenth Army attacked on the Matz River with 144 tanks in mid-June; or on 28 June, when two divisions assaulted east of Villers-Cotterets; or on 3 July, when over 1,000 prisoners were taken, 'a clear sign of faltering morale in the German Army'. The British First Army carried out a small attack near Ypres in June. And Foch had long been planning the massive counterstroke on the Marne that he unleashed on 18 July. This was the battle that influenced Allied thinking in the manner Monash attributed to Hamel.[3]

Lessons

Nevertheless, Monash did not overstate the case in saying that a steady stream of commanders and staff officers from other corps and armies in the BEF arrived at Bertangles to study the methods he had employed. GHQ included his orders in two instructional pamphlets it published on the battle. Their analysis penetrated to the core of the success, attributing it to:

(a) The care and skill as regards every detail with which the plan was drawn up by the Corps, Divisional, Brigade and Battalion Staffs.

(b) The excellent co-operation between the infantry, machine

gunners, tanks and R.A.F.

(c) The complete surprise of the enemy, resulting from the manner in which the operation had been kept secret up till zero hour.

(d) The precautions that were taken and successfully carried out by which no warning was given to the enemy by any previous activity which was not normal.

(e) The effective counter-battery work and accurate barrage.

(f) The skill and dash with which the tanks were handled and the care taken over the details in bringing them to the starting line.

(g) Last, but most important of all, the skill, determination and fine fighting spirit of the infantry carrying out the attack.

But if GHQ had thoroughly grasped the texture, it saw the battle, initially at least, as something of an aberration, issuing a caveat that warned:

It is important, in drawing deductions from this action, to bear in mind the local and special conditions, especially the high moral of the infantry, the fact that there was not much wire, that the ground was suitable for the action of tanks, and that the

Villers-Bretonneux plateau viewed from the German lines.

objective was strictly limited, and within the effective fire of the field and heavy artillery as sited for the attack.[4]

Brigadier Shelford Bidwell, a distinguished historian with vast active service experience, remarked acidly of this conclusion that 'It might have been thought that the correct deduction was that here were the principles of war being brilliantly applied'.[5] He had a point. Many of the conditions were not 'local and special' at all. Keeping objectives limited and within the artillery's protective embrace had been a guiding principle of attacks throughout 1917. The suitability of the ground for tanks had nothing to do with the particular geology of the Hamel area but everything to do with the elimination of the long preparatory bombardment that would have ripped it up. Regarding the Australians' morale, the implication seems to have been that only they could pull off the attack and that high morale was the exception rather the rule in the BEF at the time.

There was not much wire because at Hamel as elsewhere, the Germans had hastily occupied posts and localities after their own offensive stalled. Understrength and subjected to nightly shelling and bombing, they had no chance to develop continuous trenches. But the terrain offered some compensation. On 10 July, Major Burford Sampson, DSO, for whom Hamel was the latest fight in a wartime career that began at Gallipoli with 15 Battalion, walked over the battlefield that had cost his unit so dearly:

Had a good look around Vaire Wood and Central Copse. Hun position one of great natural strength – splendid field of fire and well concealed. Three distinct fire positions and numerous M.W. [Minenwerfer, the German trench mortar] emplacements. Great quantities of M.G. ammo.[6]

True, many Germans, worn down by the nightly harassment, surrendered readily or fled the attack. But those on the main front had withstood reasonably well the 'peaceful penetration' that preceded it and pockets of them fought stubbornly when it came. The Fourth Army War Diary was not the only account to describe hard fighting around Vaire and Hamel Woods and around the village.[7] On the Wolfsberg, 202 IR pressed home a vigorous counterattack that temporarily regained part of the position. Brigadier General Wisdom may have deprecated the prisoners he saw from 137 IR but its soldiers counterattacked through a storm of artillery and machine gun fire to give 25 Battalion on the right flank some very nasty moments. The prisoners Sergeant Bruce Rainsford saw were 'well equipped, in good condition and of a very good type'.[8]

A machine gun captured in house-to-house fighting in Hamel. (AWM E02669)

Moreover, the defence did not rest with the riflemen. Aware of their shortcomings, the Germans relied instead on the quantity and quality of their machine gunners. The number of machine guns captured, 177, was enough for one per forty yards of front attacked. From positions sited to take every advantage of the ground, they frequently held up the advance and inflicted most of the 1,400 casualties the attacking infantry suffered, one fifth of their strength. Every report spoke highly of the gunners' courage and tenacity in fighting to the very last. The Tank Corps War Diary gives many instances. In one, a tank destroyed a nest of six machine guns by running over it when the crews refused to surrender. In another, the machine gun was firing even as the tank trampled it. After the battle, twenty-six machine guns were dug out of a single stretch of trench that just one tank had crushed.[9]

From Monash down, the Australians recognised the massive edge the tanks had given them over the German machine guns. Tanks returning with cheering wounded and 'Dinkum Chum', 'Humdinger' and other nicknames chalked on their sides testified eloquently to the revolution in the infantry's opinion of them. The commanders of the battalions shattered at Bullecourt led this new respect. Lieutenant Colonel Marks of 13 Battalion enthused that the tanks 'even appeared to anticipate the infantry's desires'; Lieutenant Colonel McSharry in the 15th remarked of one tank that it 'saved us a great number of casualties at the final objective. This tank gave an ideal illustration of co-operation with infantry'; Lieutenant Colonel Drake-Brockman of 16 Battalion thought the tanks 'particularly useful and efficient'. GHQ noted that 'The value of tanks in assisting infantry to advance was conclusively proved'.[10]

That sentence made the point that while tanks and infantry had shared the battlefield since they advanced together up the main street of Flers in September 1916, Hamel saw the first use of tanks *with* infantry rather than tanks *and* infantry.[11] From the very start of the planning, they were to be the principal means of reducing infantry losses, which meant intimate co-operation. Both arms found the rehearsals at Vaux-en-Amienois very useful but they forged many of the techniques for working together during the battle itself. Without the tanks, Courage maintained, the infantry would have suffered severely

H52, one of three tanks disabled in the fight for Hamel. Captain Moran's tricolour flies from the house. (AWM E03843)

or been unable to advance at all. The Australians might not have been so forthright but they would not have disagreed either, as the comments from 4 Brigade's battalion commanders showed. J.F.C. Fuller thought that the reputation of the Tank Corps owed more to Hamel than Cambrai.[12]

Although they had vigorously opposed it during the planning, the tank commanders admitted afterwards that their infantry counterparts were right about the creeping barrage. Besides protecting the tanks from anti-tank rifles, Courage wrote, 'it prevents hostile machine gunners from taking aimed fire and thus gives the Tank an equal chance of gaining superiority of fire'. The German machine gunners had to survive in turn the pre-zero hour harassing fire, the creeping barrage and finally a combined tank and infantry assault. Their chances were slim as long as all these means of subduing them were employed. When they were not, the infantry had to assault in the old way with the usual results.[13] Pear Trench, which largely escaped the barrage and the tanks missed altogether, cost the Australians almost half the battalion allotted to take it.

As tanks could move closer to the barrage than the infantry and

Well-constructed dugouts in the bank of the sunken road at Pear Trench. (AWM E02708)

Soldiers from 43 Battalion on a ruined street in Hamel. (AWM E02668)

actually underneath it if shrapnel were being used, Courage recommended that henceforth they should lead the infantry. Reflecting its damascene conversion after the attack, the 4th Australian Division wholeheartedly agreed:

> The power of tanks to lean closely on the Artillery barrage renders it unnecessary for Infantry to do so as closely as has been the practice. This should mean a considerable reduction of casualties both from enemy action on the lifting of the artillery barrage and from the inevitable short rounds from our own Artillery. It will also have a very desirable effect of automatically clearing passages through any enemy wire that may exist.[14]

For this reason, too, Courage recommended a later zero hour because light enough for the tanks to find their way was still too gloomy for them to use their guns effectively.

Courage was unstinting in his admiration of the Australians, stating that 'all Tank Officers were much impressed that they never considered that the presence of the Tanks exonerated them from fighting, and took instant advantage of any opportunity created by the Tanks'.[15] Before the tanks caught up or whenever a tank was not to hand, the GHQ reports noted, the Australians fought their way forward making full use of their own weapons, especially the bayonet and bomb. The standard

An aerial photo taken after the battle showing the effects of intense shelling of Hamel and the Wolfsberg. Compare this picture with the one on p. 44.

of infantry platoon leading was especially praised, a tribute to the Australian system of promoting veterans from the ranks. An Australian private taking over an American platoon after its leaders were hit typified the individual initiative that attracted comment. C.E.W. Bean was adamant that the battle would have ended differently without first-class infantry.[16]

As for the Americans, Rawlinson waxed lyrically that they 'fought like tigers', Monash said they 'acquitted themselves most gallantly' and the Australian infantry praised them as well, though observing that they had the fault of all first class fighting men who lack experience – excessive keenness.[17] The Americans went into the battle as half-trained infantry that had almost never been near the front line. Despite their enthusiasm, they were beset by indecision, particularly if their commanders fell, and they tended to bunch, resulting in heavy casualties from a single shell. They invariably took their lead from the Australians. Alongside them, men like Pope and Zyburt certainly did fight like tigers. The 13 Battalion History recounts an amusing episode on this theme:

'I guess we're shark troops now,' one of a party of Yanks visiting us after Hamel remarked.

Thinking he was referring to collecting souvenirs from Fritzs, and not being willing to take second or even equal place with anyone at that, our 'Souvenir King' took out a heap of German watches, marks, photos, soldbuchs, feldpostbriefs, revolvers and daggers, and proudly retorted, 'You'll have to be Some Shark Troops to beat that little heap, I guess, Guy.'

'I wasn't referring to souvenirs, Aussie. I said I guess after that battle we'll be regarded as shark troops like you Australians. Shark Troops – SHARK Troops like you. S-H-O-C-K – shark troops.' The Digger's perplexed look vanished.[18]

The artillery expended over 200,000 shells in firing the creeping and protective barrages, the harassing and counterbattery programmes, and the various SOS shoots. It relied heavily on target information provided by 5 Brigade's aircraft. Together with the guns, they protected both tanks and infantry by engaging German artillery and infantry at the first sign of their coming into action. Aerial attacks badly dislocated the counterattack on the Wolfsberg. And by camouflaging the tanks' approach, aircraft removed the Germans' best chance of detecting the attack. Tanks, artillery, aircraft – each was an essential part of the maximum array of mechanical resources helping the infantry forward.

A Little Masterpiece

Though the co-operation between the tanks and infantry received the most attention, all four arms had been brilliantly co-ordinated on the battlefield. Indeed, Elles regarded Hamel as 'certainly the most successfully executed small battle of all arms' within his experience. Putting it another way, Bean called Hamel 'a big battle on a small scale because all the appurtenances of a big battle were used'. The closeness between conception and execution led Monash to coin the famous analogy: 'A perfected modern battle plan is like nothing so much as a score for an orchestral composition, where the various arms and units are the instruments, and the tasks they perform are their respective musical phrases'.[19]

Monash was the conductor. Hamel exemplified a tactical approach that gave the infantry every conceivable assistance and did not commit them to assaults on distant objectives that they would reach too weak to hold. Regretting that he was not strong on invention himself, Monash took the ideas of Elles and Courage, and lesser innovations such as the parachuting of ammunition, and applied them with his engineer's mind to the problem at hand as though they were materials being assembled at a site. So that their confidence would not be dented, he deferred to his commanders' misgivings over the relegation of the artillery, though the underlying concept of the attack changed radically as a result. Conferences addressed the smallest detail, eliminating confusion and uncertainty. As even the most lavish support could not guarantee success if the attack were compromised, the effort to deceive and surprise was unsparing.

General Monash, architect of the success at Hamel.

The attack did not make Monash the first exponent of blitzkrieg as some of his admirers have rather absurdly claimed. Yes, strongly held features were left for specially designated battalions and companies to clear while the advance went around them. But the Blue Line enclosed a strictly limited objective. Many Australians felt that the attack should have gone at least as far as the German gun line and that stopping short was a waste of effort. Courage wanted the Protective Barrage pushed farther out to give the tanks room to exploit. Monash would have none of it. As the attack was effectively an experiment, he wanted to maximise the chances of success and opted for what seemed possible, rather than being seduced by what seemed desirable. Nothing like Guderian's armoured thrusts across France and Russia in 1940-41 was intended. Blitzkrieg would have to wait for the next war.

Hamel raised the technique employed at Cambrai to its final stage of development. It was the model for the much bigger and better known offensive astride the Somme on August 8, 1918, which Ludendorff famously called 'the black day of the German Army', and, in fact, all infantry/tank attacks in the BEF until the armistice.[20] Hamel was, therefore, a significant battle but it has been largely overlooked in recent years except in Australia, where the Royal United Services Institute of New South Wales held a major seminar in 1998 that examined every aspect. It has also been diminished by the claim that all battles were fought in the same way by 1918. They were – after Hamel. As the prolific First World War historian John Terraine has written, Hamel was 'a revolution, a textbook victory, a little masterpiece casting a long shadow before it'.[21]

NOTES

1. *AV*, p. 56.
2. J.J. Pershing, *My Experiences in the World War,* (Harper & Row, 1932), p. 475.
3. *AV*, pp. 44, 64; J. Terraine, *To Win a War* (Sidgwick & Jackson, 1978), p.85; Pedersen, *Monash*, p. 233.
4. 'GHQ Notes on Recent Fighting No. 19', 5 August 1918; SS218, 'Notes Compiled by GS Fourth Army on the Operation of the Australian Corps Against Hamel on 4 July', MC.
5. R.G.S. Bidwell, *Gunners at War* (Arms and Armour Press, 1970), p. 41.
6. Entry for 10 July 1918, *Burford Sampson Great War Diary* (privately published by Richard G. Sampson, 1997), p.149.
7. Fourth Army War D, 4 July 1918, Item 350/8, AWM 26.
8. Cited in Laffin, *Hamel*, p. 99.
9. HQ Tank Corps War D, 6 July 1918, Item 358/17, AWM 26.
10. G. Blaxland, *Amiens 1918* (W.H. Allen, 1981), p. 149; *OH. VI*, p.328; McSharry's narrative, Appendix 3 to 15 Battalion War D, July 1918, Item 23/47, Roll 47, AWM 4.
11. Beaumont, op. cit., p. 16.
12. J.F.C. Fuller, *Memoirs of an Unconventional Soldier* (Nicholson & Watson, 1936), pp. 287-90.
13. R. Prior and T. Wilson, *Command on the Western Front* (Blackwell, 1992), pp. 298-300.
14. 4th Australian Division, 'Hamel Offensive Lessons', c. 6 July 1918, Item 408/5, AWM 26.
15. '5 Tank Brigade After Action Report'; Tank Corps Headquarters, 'Lecture on the History of the British Tank Corps', 3 September 1918, AWRS 925/4, AWM.
16. *OH. VI*, p. 329.
17. Rawlinson to Wigram, 7 July 1918, Item 5201/33/73, Rawlinson Collection; *AV*, p. 59; See also Report on Operations, 8 July 1918, Appendix 1 to 13 Battalion War D, July 1918, Item 23/30, Roll 45, AWM 4; Huntingdon, op cit.
18. White, op. cit, pp. 146-7.
19. Elles in *OH. VI*, p. 334; C.E.W. Bean, 'Narrative of 1918', MC: *AV*, p. 56.
20. Maj-Gen. E.K.G. Sixsmith, *British Generalship in the Twentieth Century* (Arms and Armour Press, 1970), p. 140.
21. Terraine, *Haig*, p. 450; *To Win a War*, pp. 85, 89.

Chapter Six

CEMETERIES AND MEMORIALS

Whereas cemeteries dot the 1916 battlefields north of the Somme, the Hamel battlefield south of the river has none. The earlier battles, such as High Wood, Thiepval, Pozières and Serre were so costly and protracted that they spawned permanent cemeteries, some of them eponymously named. Hamel, by contrast, was over so quickly and cost so little that the dead were interred in existing cemeteries or in small battlefield plots from which they were gathered into concentration cemeteries after the war. The remains of those killed during Peaceful Penetration and the attacks around Ville-sur-Ancre and Morlancourt in May and June 1918 were handled in the same way.

Adelaide Cemetery

About 14 kilometres from Amiens and on the left of the N29 just before it crosses the railway bridge on the western outskirts of Villers-Bretonneux, Adelaide Cemetery was begun in June 1918 near an advanced dressing station. It was used by the 2nd and 3rd Australian Divisions until the advance of 8 August carried the line eastwards. Plot 1, with its mixed Australian and British graves, is the site of the original cemetery.

After the Armistice, 864 graves from nearby Embankment and Chalk Lane Cemeteries and White Chateau and Cachy British Cemeteries outside the village of Cachy, were concentrated at Adelaide Cemetery. Of the 954 burials, 519 are Australian, all of whom fell between March and September 1918. The majority were grouped in Plot III, which comprises the graves of 426 Australians, an English soldier and an unknown. Of the rest, 365 are British, 22 Canadian and 48 unknown.

In 1993 the remains of an unknown Australian soldier were exhumed from grave III.M.13 and, in a poignant nationally televised ceremony on November 11, reinterred as the 'Unknown Australian Soldier' in the Hall of Memory, the most

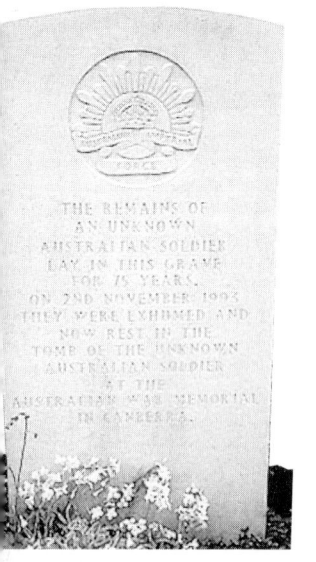

Adelaide Cemetery. The headstone on the plot from which the Unknown Australian Soldier was taken.

sacred part of the Australian War Memorial in Canberra. A special headstone stands over the gravesite now.

Aubigny British Cemetery

North of the D1 at the entrance to Aubigny, the cemetery is in the area where 4 Brigade rested and the tanks assembled before the attack. Begun and used by 14 and 15 Brigades from the 5th Australian Division between April and August 1918, it contains the graves of 88 Australians and seven British gunners.

Beacon Cemetery

On the D1 about 800 metres west of its junction with the D42 from Morlancourt, this cemetery is named after the Brick Beacon, the tall brick chimney that stood in the fields nearby, crowning the summit of the Morlancourt Ridge. Established by the 18th (British) Division on 15 August for the graves of 109 men killed in the attack a week before, it became a postwar concentration cemetery. Of the 768 burials, 195 are Australian. Some of the 58 unknowns probably fell in the diversionary raid that 55 Battalion launched 750 metres to the southeast. Extending across the Ancre to Albert and Thiepval, the northward vista is panoramic. A short walk along the track that runs southwards from the cemetery opens up good views across the Somme to the Wolfsberg.

Crucifix Corner Cemetery

Sixty Hamel dead rest in this cemetery, which is just over two kilometres south of Villers-Bretonneux on the D23. They include Lieutenant Ramsay Wood from 14 Battalion at X.C.5 and Company Sergeant Major George Hunt, DCM, a well-known soldier from 21 Battalion, at IX.A.22. Largely overlooked today, Crucifix Corner is an important cemetery as much of the fighting in the counterattack that recaptured Villers-Bretonneux on 25 April 1918 took place around the site.

Crucifix Corner Cemetery.

It is also where the Canadians attacked on 8 August. They started the cemetery after that battle but it closed the same month. When it reopened as a postwar concentration cemetery, 28 Australians from a temporary cemetery near the western side of Vaire Wood were among the Hamel fallen reinterred there.

On Crucifix Corner closing, it held 656 burials, of which 236 were Australian and another 60 Australian unknowns. They outnumber the 76 Canadians, who now form most of Plot 1. Almost the entire left side of the cemetery is given over to 142 French graves, which face east like the British graves alongside them, symbolising the joint effort of the two armies to stem the German advance in the spring of 1918 before launching the advance to victory from the area in the summer.

Daours Communal Cemetery Extension

As Daours was on the Amiens-Albert railway line, five casualty clearing stations were set up around it before the Somme offensive of 1916. Although the cemetery was used in the offensive, two thirds of the 1,224 burials are from 1918. Most of the 458 Australians died between May and September that year. They represent more AIF units and more battles than the Australian dead of any other cemetery. Among the Hamel casualties are Captain Frederick Woods and Company Sergeant Major Harold Blinman of 16 Battalion. Both were hit by fire from a machine gun that was subsequently knocked out by Lance Corporal Thomas Axford in an exploit that won him the Victoria Cross. Second Lieutenant Horace Blee, who was wounded in the same action, also rests in Daours. Woods, Blinman and Blee were all good friends and had been sergeants major of D Company. Woods is buried at III.D.37 with Blee and Blinman either side.

Behind the Cross of Sacrifice is a plot containing Indian soldiers and Chinese labourers. Some of the Indians belonged to the Deccan Horse and died from wounds sustained in the cavalry action at High Wood on 14 July 1916. The long, narrow cemetery is on the D115 at the northern edge of the village.

Dive Copse Cemetery

About two kilometres north of Sailly-Laurette on the road to Treux, this cemetery was used by the field ambulances concentrated in the area before the 1916 offensive. They eventually became the XIV Corps Main Dressing Station, whose commanding officer lent his name to the small wood 800 metres north on the D1. In turn, the wood lent its name to the cemetery. Plots I and II contain the graves of men who died of wounds during the first three months of the 1916 campaign and comprise almost 70% of the 579 burials. Plot III consists of graves from the 1918 fighting, 53 of which are Australian. Many of these men belonged to 18 Battalion and were casualties of the attack on Ville on 19 May. Six are commemorated to the right of the Stone of Remembrance because their whereabouts in the cemetery are unknown. The southward view towards Hamel is outstanding.

Fouilloy Communal Cemetery

Fouilloy and its environs served as a tank forward assembly area. The 38 graves in the cemetery, which is on the D1 at the western edge of the village, date from early 1918, when No. 53 Casualty Clearing Station and No. 41 Stationary Hospital were established there. Twelve are British, one is Canadian and the rest Australian. Though they are not of Hamel fallen, two graves reflect unusual deaths. Major Cyril Seelenmeyer, MC, of the Australian Army Veterinary Corps, died of wounds received while tending injured artillery horses on August 8. Private W. Montgomery of the British Army Service Corps drowned in September while swimming in the Somme.

Mericourt-l'Abbé Communal Cemetery Extension

On the left of the D120 as it leaves Méricourt for Treux and short of its junction with the D119, this cemetery served the medical units clustered around the nearby railway line from the summer of 1915 until July 1916. It reopened between March and August 1918 and was also used postwar for the burial of unidentified dead. Of the 407 graves, 122 are Australian and they comprise most of the 1918 casualties. By a quirk of fate, they include a remarkable number of men who were decorated as non-commissioned officers and then commissioned. Second Lieutenant Stephen Facey, DCM and Belgian Croix de Guerre, from 59 Battalion, and Lieutenant John Moore, MC and Bar, MM, of 60 Battalion died of wounds received during the Hamel diversions and rest at III.E.1 and III.E.3 respectively. Another Hamel casualty, Lieutenant J.R. Ranson of 8 Trench Mortar Battery, lies between them.

Villers-Bretonneux Military Cemetery and Australian National Memorial

Half way between Villers-Bretonneux and Fouilloy on the eastern side of the D23, the cemetery was established after the war to concentrate the dead from, among others, Card Copse and Midway Cemeteries at Marcelcave, Dury Hospital Military Cemetery, High and

Kangaroo Cemeteries at Sailly-le-Sec, Lamotte-en-Santerre and Vaux-sur-Somme Communal Cemeteries and Le Hamelet British Cemetery. Covering the period March-August 1918, Plots I to XX contain the majority of the 779 Australian graves and were completed by 1920. Plots IIIA, VIA, XIIIA and XVIA and the AA rows inside the boundaries of the central lawn were made by 1925. With the graves of 1089 British soldiers, 267 Canadians, 4 South Africans and 2 New Zealanders as well as the Australians, the cemetery is the largest on the 1918 battlefield.

The Australian National Memorial, Villers-Bretonneux.

Dedicated by King George VI in July 1938, the Australian National Memorial is at the eastern end of the cemetery and partly hidden by the convex curve of the intervening ground. The Australians chose the site because it was the setting for their leading role in the two famous counterattacks that regained Villers-Bretonneux – and saved Amiens – in April 1918. A British general who saw their bayonet charge in bright moonlight across this ground called it 'perhaps the greatest individual feat of the war', and Marshal Foch referred to the Australians' 'altogether astonishing valiance'.

Sir Edward Lutyens' design features a bell tower 100 feet high and flanked by screen walls that enshrine the names of the 10,982 Australians killed in France (except for the 1,298 listed at VC Corner Cemetery at Fromelles) but who have no known grave. Private Thomas Parrish of 13 Battalion, killed while guiding a tank; Private James Lynch, the club wielding giant from 44 Battalion who fell after routing the Germans during their counterattack on the Wolfsberg; Lieutenant Louis Stafford, shot during 55 Battalion's diversion at the Brick Beacon; and Corporal Edwin Skinner, who died in 58 Battalion's sortie on the Ancre, are all commemorated on the panels.

The Memorial was damaged in June 1940 when a German tank crashed through the lower right hand corner of the cemetery and engaged a French machine gun crew in the tower, which a Bf 109 also strafed for good measure. Spalling on the Cross of Sacrifice and some of the headstones remain as honourable scars of war. The tower offers excellent views in every direction, although Hill 104 to the east masks much of the low ground between the Australian line and Hamel village. If it is not open, the keys can be obtained from the gendarmerie. A ceremony is held annually at the Memorial on Anzac Day, 25 April.

The Australian Corps Memorial Park

Set among some of the original German trenches on the Wolfsberg, this memorial owes much to the late John Laffin, a prolific Australian military historian who slogged through the Second World War campaigns in New Guinea as an infantryman. Laffin admired the memorial parks created by the Canadians at Vimy, the Newfoundlanders at Beaumont-Hamel and the South Africans at Delville Wood and the British Memorial to the Missing at Thiepval, each on ground made sacred by their soldiers' blood. He was acutely aware – and embarrassed – that Australia had nothing similar to commemorate the war service and sacrifice of its own soldiers. Thus began a 40-year crusade as Laffin lobbied a governor-general, four prime ministers, ex-servicemen's organizations and church leaders. They all liked the idea but took it no further.

Laffin was especially disappointed by the political response – or lack of it. 'Politicians', he wrote, 'from prime ministers down to lowly backbenchers, saw no votes in a new type of memorial 12,000 miles from home'.[1] Not until 1996, when the Hon. Bruce Scott became Minister of Veterans' Affairs and Air-Vice Marshal Alan Heggen was Director of the Office of Australian War Graves, did the project really move forward. The French Government donated the ground for the actual memorial area and it was opened on 4 July 1998, the 70th anniversary of the battle, by Scott and his French counterpart, M. Jean-Pierre Massaret. Scott's great uncle, Ken Bassett, fought at Hamel with 15 Battalion after surviving Pozières, Bullecourt, Passchendaele and Villers-Bretonneux. Scott also paid tribute to Laffin, who lived long enough to see his vision realised.

The Australian Corps Memorial on the Wolfsberg above Hamel.

Hamel Wood   Vaire Wood

Original trenches on the Wolfsberg in the Australian Corps Memorial Park.

The Memorial consists of three curved walls of black granite, into which Melbourne stonemason Colin Anderson sandblasted the Australian Rising Sun badge, a likeness of Monash, scenes from the battle, Clemenceau's speech after it and Ludendorff's comment about August 8 being the German Army's black day. Colour patches from every AIF unit have been glazed onto the top of the low encompassing walls and glass information panels in the trenches explain significant points in English and French. Unfortunately, the Memorial's remoteness has made it an easy target for vandals. They have repeatedly smashed the glass panels and damaged the toilets. Poor finishing has let rain seep behind many of the granite tiles, lifting them off when the water freezes during the winter. A major refurbishment has already taken place. Random security checks have also been instituted.

Ceremonies are held on July 4 or, if that day falls during the week, on the first weekend after. At some point, the eyes of those attending and, indeed, of anyone who comes here, are drawn to the tablet at the base of the granite walls. Conversation ceases and emotion-tinged reflection starts as the immortal words that C.E.W. Bean penned at the close of his epic Official History are read:

What these men did nothing can alter now. The good and the bad, the greatness and the smallness of their story will stand. Whatever of glory it contains nothing now can lessen. It rises, as it will always rise, above the mists of ages, a monument to great-hearted men; and, for their nation, a possession forever.[2]

NOTES

1. Laffin, *Hamel*, p.15. This chapter has also drawn on M. and M. Middlebrook, *The Somme Battlefields* (Viking, 1991).
2. *OH. VI*, p. 1096.

Chapter Seven

BATTLEFIELD TOURS

As the Hamel area lacks the emotional resonance of the 1916 battlefields around Albert, it is relatively unvisited, which is a pity. The Advance to Victory began at Hamel, and in many ways with the battle. Because the fighting was not static, the ground remained largely intact. Crops and tall grass covered it in mid-1918 just as they do in mid-year now. The modern IGN maps fit over the old trench maps like templates, making the battle easy to follow. With a population of 600, Hamel itself is leafy, quiet, sleepy even, which is totally in character with this stretch of the Somme. The beauty, tranquillity and glorious views in the valley and on the heights above the river, the old world charm of Corbie, with its two magnificent churches, and the scenery along the Ancre valley all make driving, cycling or walking something to savour, particularly during the long, warm, lazy summer days. Battlefield touring does not get any better than this.

Hamel. Place du 8 Mai 1945.

The Wolfsberg

Most places on the battlefield can easily be identified from the Australian Corps Memorial Park, which stands on the site of the German command post on the Wolfsberg. As the Memorial can also be seen from so much of the battlefield, it serves as an excellent orientation point for every tour and walk. The Wolfsberg, too, was the scene of sharp fighting and the main German riposte. Given its importance, a description of the feature and the views from it would seem appropriate at the outset.

The Wolfsberg is at the northern tip of a finger spur of the Villers-Bretonneux plateau. Accroche Wood is due south on this spur and the wooded area to the southwest is the conjoined mass of Hamel and Vaire Woods. The Australian line, from which 4 and 11 Brigades attacked, followed the road along the crest of the next spur to the west, which is crowned by Mouse Copse. At the time of writing a big pile of white ballast on the verge made the road easy to spot. The German line skirted Hamel, headed west to join the sunken road that ran along the facing side of the spur, then swung around the far side of Vaire Wood. Pear Trench was almost due west on this road. Kidney Trench abutted Central Copse, the untidy outgrowth at the tip of Vaire Wood. The tower of the Australian National Memorial is on the skyline but Hill 104 hides the rest of it.

Putting yourself in the position of 3/202 RIR and the artillery observers here, look west. Notice how the far spur line blocks the view, so that the tanks could assemble behind it without your seeing them and, because of the din from the aircraft above you, without your hearing them. Their Jumping Off Line ran along the spur just in front of Mouse Copse but they moved to it in darkness and this time the noise patrol aircraft were bombing you as well. Your stunned surprise

Panorama from the Wolfsberg showing the German line and the ground over which the Australians attacked towards Hamel.

Looking north along the Blue Line from the Wolfsberg. Accroche Wood (l), Hamel Wood (r).

is hardly to be wondered at!

Now follow the spur from Mouse Copse down to the Somme. The village of Hamelet is at the river's edge. Some tanks were concealed in the orchards around it and the rest at Fouilloy, which is completely hidden. The twin towers of St Pierre Church rise above Corbie on the far side. Vaire is northwest of you on the near bank and Bouzencourt, just a few buildings and easily missed, is at the end of the northerly road from Hamel to the river. Both front lines started at Bouzencourt, but the Australian trenches passed in front of Vaire, across the flats and up the far spur, while the German line cut straight to Hamel.

The 55 Battalion feints were on the high ground above Sailly-Laurette, which you can see across the Somme to the northeast. Note how far the Australians on the northern bank had advanced past their line on the southern and how German guns around Accroche Wood could fire into their rear. Note, too, the terrific views the Germans had

from the Wolfsberg and the vulnerability of infantry advancing over the open ground to the west.

As the walk from the car park to the Memorial makes abundantly clear, the Wolfsberg was not a small position. Part of the old Amiens Defence Line, it was 550 metres across and sown with deep dugouts. The northern extremity lay well to the north of the access road and, on the western side, the trenches reached about halfway down to Hamel. 44 Battalion and its twelve tanks attacked up this slope and crushed many trenches on the crest. The eastern edge, along which the Blue Line ran, was in the scrubby fringe beyond the trench at the end of the car park. 1/202 RIR's counterattack was stopped in this area before an assault, heroically led by Private James Lynch from the direction of the Memorial, broke it. Pursued by the Australians and some Americans, the Germans fled into the Vallée d'Abancourt from whence they had come.

TOUR ONE: SOUTH OF THE SOMME. THE MAIN ATTACK

This tour covers the attack by 4, 6 and 11 Brigades, the 7 Brigade diversion, the tank and infantry assembly and forming up areas and the cemeteries on the southern bank of the Somme. It represents a considerable expansion of the tour in the 1918 battlefield tour package produced by the Australian Department of Veterans' Affairs. Some of the checkpoints on that tour are mentioned in this one.

Leave the Australian Corps Memorial Park (**1**) and **turn left** at the T-junction on reaching Hamel. After half a kilometre, stop at the Chapelle St. Roche (**2**), which is on the left of the road and signposted as Checkpoint 14. While 43 Battalion cleared Hamel and half of 44 Battalion skirted the northern side of the village, the other half of 44 Battalion swept around the southern side and up this slope to the Blue Line, which ran along the southern shoulder of the Wolfsberg 600 metres east of the chapel. 44 Battalion's twelve supporting tanks were distributed evenly along this frontage.

The trench in P.10.d, which held up 15 Battalion's advance to the Blue Line after the barrage resumed, extended from the high ground in rear towards Accroche Wood. Fifty Germans and twenty-seven machine guns were captured when a tank drove along it hugged by the infantry. Before reaching this trench, 15 Battalion attacked past the near side of Vaire and Hamel Woods, which you can see on gently rising ground a kilometre to the southwest. The Germans made a last ditch stand in the northeast corner of Hamel Wood, which is facing you. Ammunition drop zones and dumping points for carrier tanks

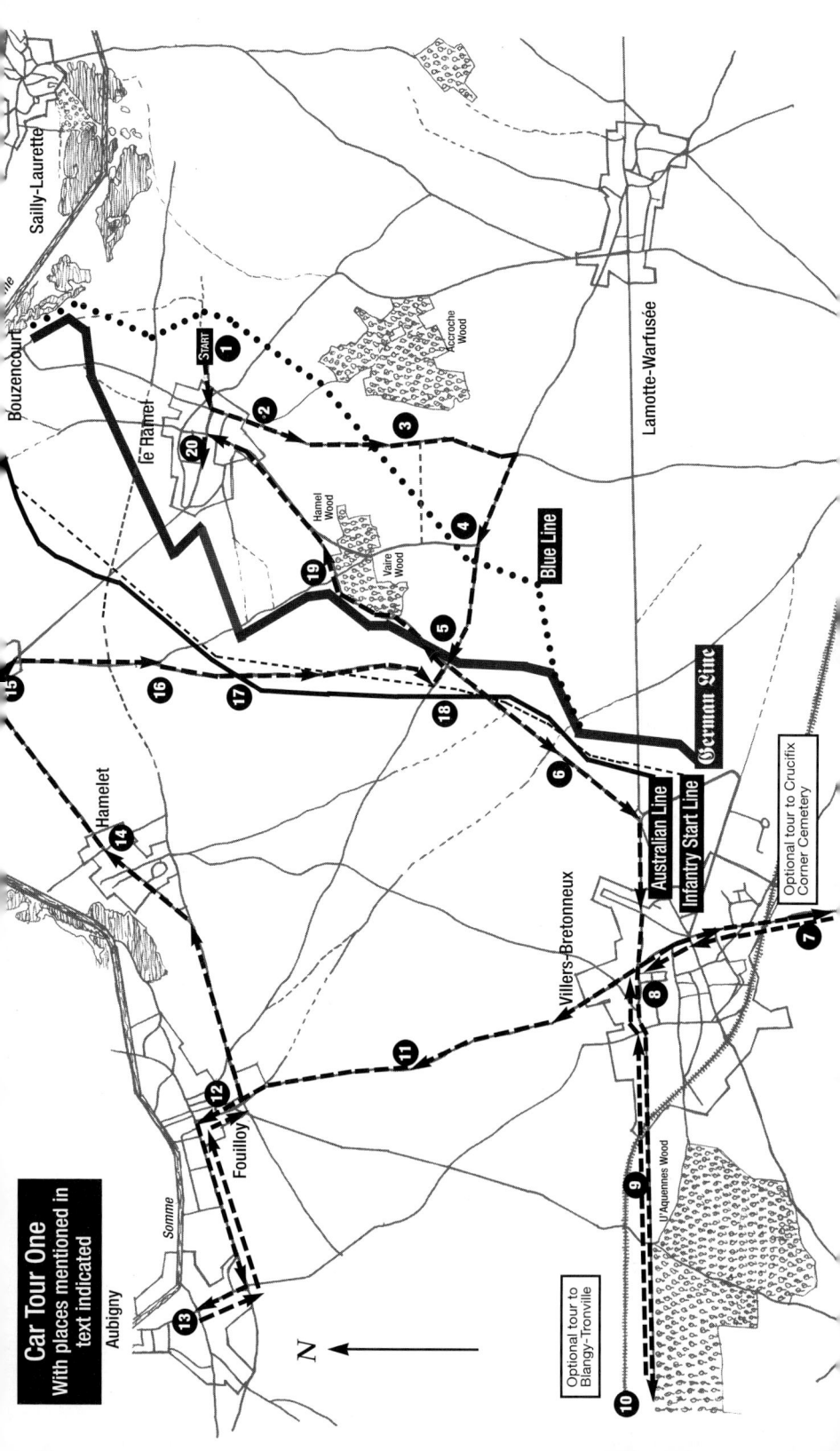

Car Tour One
With places mentioned in text indicated

were in the areas between the chapel and the woods on one side and the Wolfsberg on the other. D Company from 14 Battalion took 15 prisoners while digging the northern end of the support line just to the east of the chapel.

Continue south for 750 metres, keeping a lookout for Checkpoint 13. Hun's Walk, linking Hamel and Accroche Woods and which 13 and 55 IR used as an escape route, crossed the road at this point as did the Blue Line. It was also the boundary between 13 and 15 Battalions. Parking is not easy here so you may find it more convenient to stop at the junction with the east-west farm track 300 metres further on (**3**). Trenches from the German support line were scattered along the sides of the road in this area. Ration Row, which should have been occupied by A Company from 13 Battalion and caused such problems for Lieutenant Rule's platoon, was in the field 200 metres west. Lieutenant Ramsay Wood was sniped there. The proximity of Accroche Wood illustrates Monash's conception of Hamel as a limited attack. Many Australians thought afterwards that he should have set the Blue Line further east.

Turn right onto the D122 after 900 metres. A minor road meets it on the right 750 metres further on (**4**). This junction is 100 metres short of P.21.a.4.0, the boundary between 4 and 6 Brigades and where the Blue Line crossed the D122, while the Protective Barrage Line crossed it 270 metres behind you. The minor road heads north to bisect the two

Post battle aerial photo that shows how the Blue Line stopped well short of Accroche Wood. The Wolfsberg is out of picture on the left.

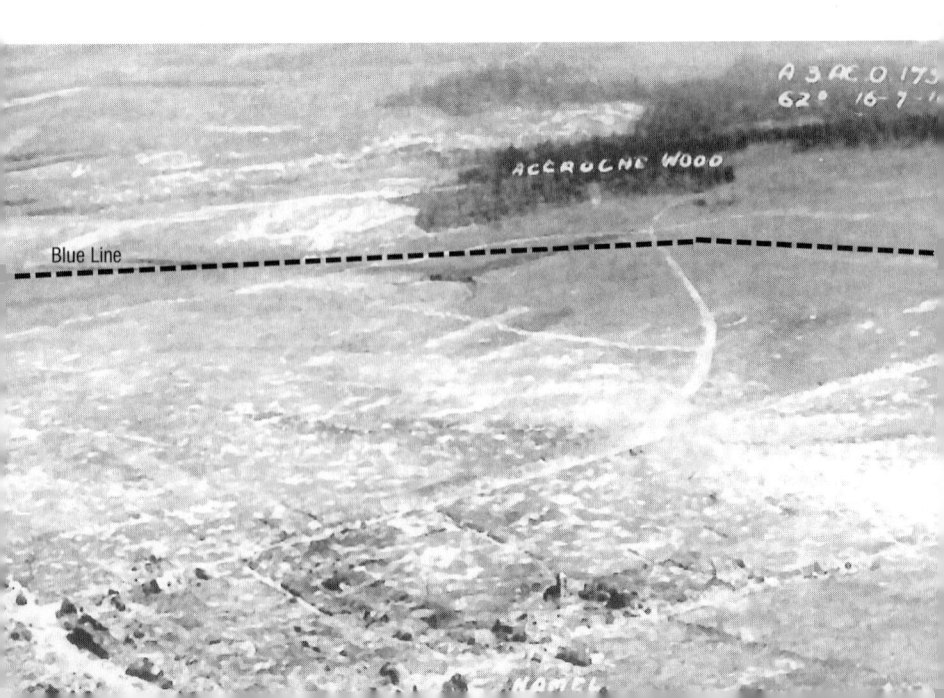

woods, and the machine guns that pinned Captain Marper's company down and severely wounded him while he signalled a tank were on the right hand side just before it entered them. An ammunition drop zone and a carrier tank dumping point were located near the road about half way to the woods.

When you **reach the intersection** with the Hamel to Villers-Bretonneux road after another kilometre (**5**), you will be on the German front line at P.20.a.5.5. Held by 13 and 15 IR, it ran along the right side of the Hamel road for 200 metres before crossing over and continuing around the front of Vaire Wood, which is to your north east. 13 Battalion's Start Line ran northward past the crossroads 180 metres to your north west. It attacked between your location and the edge of the wood, dropping off companies as it went. The scrubby depression between the two lines was a small quarry in which the Germans had a post. Formerly a peaceful penetration objective, it lay directly under the Barrage Line and was obliterated along with the surrounding trenches.

Leave the D122 and take the road to Villers-Bretonneux, which crosses the plateau on 6 Brigade's frontage. Its trenches and the Start Line were up to 180 metres east of this road. The flat, open ground was ideal for tanks and the attack unfolded effortlessly as they flattened everything in their path. Most of the 9.2-inch shelling to create craters for the infantry to use as cover was in this area. Stop after 1.5 kilometres and look eastwards (**6**). You are now on the boundary between 23 Battalion on your left and 25 Battalion from 7 Brigade on your right. Their Start Line was 150 metres east of the road here and the Barrage Line, Blue Line and 137 IR's front line all coincided 150 metres further east.

The resistance on this flank was fierce, particularly against 25 Battalion's diversion, which lacked tank support. B Company, advancing on the other side of the N29, had some very anxious moments when 3/137 IR counterattacked along the road from the direction of Lamotte-Warfusée, the village straddling it to the east, and from the south. D Company, which attacked between your location and the N29, sent a platoon to assist, whereupon the Germans started surrendering from as far out as 275 metres beyond the Blue Line. **Before leaving**, look northeastwards towards the tip of Hamel Wood to follow the approximate track of the Blue Line. Whereas the advance was less than 200 metres here, it had to cover a kilometre to reach the Blue Line there. The extra room the attack created on the Villers-Bretonneux plateau is self-evident.

Hamelet　　　　　　　　　　　　　　　　　　　　Mouse Copse

The view eastwards over Hill 104 from the Australian National Memorial.

Taking the **N29 into the village**, continue past the Demarcation Stone that shows the limit of the German advance in 1918 and **turn left at the D23**, which is signposted for Crucifix Corner Cemetery 2.25 kilometres away on the right of the road (**7**). You will pass over a five-way intersection and the autoroute before reaching it. Company Sergeant Major George Hunt, DCM, at IX.A.22, and Lieutenant Ramsay Wood at X.C.5 are among the Hamel fallen in this cemetery. The surrounding area figured in the counterattack that regained Villers-Bretonneux on 25 April 1918 and the Canadians attacked from it on August 8.

Return to the town (**8**) and visit the Anzac Museum in the primary school at 9 Rue Victoria. It displays an interesting collection of AIF memorabilia and the theatre screens the hour-long Australian Army documentary, *Hamel-The Turning Point*. Destroyed in April 1918, the school was rebuilt through donations from schoolchildren in the Australian state of Victoria and reopened in 1927. On 5 May 1984, Villers-Bretonneux and the Victorian town of Robinvale, both with a population of around 3,500, were twinned.

Adelaide Cemetery (**9**) is on the right of the N29 two kilometres west of Villers-Bretonneux. The remains of an unidentified Australian were exhumed from III.M.13 and reinterred as the Unknown Australian Soldier in the Hall of Memory at the Australian War Memorial on 11 November 1993. **The safest way to head back to the town is to continue a short distance towards Amiens on the N29 and turn around at the intersection with the D523.** Alternatively,

                    Hamel   Vaire Wood

you can continue for another five kilometres and turn right onto the D167 for Blangy-Tronville (**10**), where 8 Tank Battalion had its headquarters, before returning to the N29. Either way, **when you reach the D23, turn left** towards Fouilloy and follow the signs to the Australian National Memorial (**11**). Take care when parking as the blind crest makes oncoming traffic difficult to see.

The Memorial is not visible from the car park but comes into view as you walk up the hill through the cemetery, when the importance of this position during the counterattacks on the town in April 1918 becomes apparent. If the tower is not open, obtain the keys from the gendarmerie because the views are not to be missed. You can see Fouilloy, Hamelet, Hamel and Vaire Woods, the right flank south of them and, with binoculars, the Australian Corps Memorial. Hill 104, which is what military planners would call the vital ground in this area, hides the low ground in the centre of the attack.

Continue north on the D23 to Fouilloy (**12**), which was a tank forward assembly area. From here, you can turn left onto the D1, drive the few kilometres to Aubigny (**13**), where 4 Brigade rested and the tanks initially assembled, and return to Fouilloy, or **turn right onto the D623** for Hamelet (**14**). When you reach the junction of the D122 and D71 roads after 500 metres, **continue on the D71**. Park in the square opposite Hamelet church and walk to the eastern edge of the village. Hamelet was the second forward assembly area for the tanks, which were concealed in the ruins of the houses and in the surrounding orchards. Masked by the drone of the FE2bs overhead, they idled out of their hides at 10.30 pm on 3 July and headed for the Jumping Off Line, which ran past Mouse Copse, the wood crowning the height a

137

kilometre south, and down to the river. The Australian line was on the same spur but 700 metres further east.

Now head for Vaire-sous-Corbie (15), the next village on the D71. It was over two kilometres behind the Australian line, which reached the Somme at Bouzencourt. Two bridges linked Vaire to Vaux across the river. The gunners used one, a pontoon bridge that was dismantled every morning. The second, a decoy, attracted so much German artillery fire that the disgruntled commander of a battery nearby had it destroyed. Remain on the D71 as it turns sharp right at Vaire church. After 200 metres, you will see a crucifix between two trees at a fork in the road.

Take the minor road on the right for 1.5 kilometres, crossing 42 Battalion's frontage, and stop at a second fork (**16**) marked by another crucifix and a sign for Checkpoint 6. On its way to Bouzencourt, the 11 Brigade line crossed the unsealed sunken road on the left (not to be confused with the foot track that heads due east to Hamel!) 600 metres from this location. Pear Trench straddled the road another 200 metres beyond. You will have to walk to both sites. Be prepared for some serious mud if it has been raining!

Turn onto the sealed road on the right and stop after 900 metres (**17**). The roadside sign indicates Checkpoint 7 rather than P.8.c.5.4 and the big pile of chalk ballast is the one you saw from the Wolfsberg. Whereas you had the German view there, you have the Australian view here and you can improve it by climbing the chalk pile. The 4 Brigade front line, occupied by 15 Battalion, crossed the road at this point but the Start Line was in the fields 100 metres to the east. 43 Battalion was strung out on the slope up which you have just come.

Completely hidden by the convex ground, Pear Trench, where Private Henry Dalziel won the Victoria Cross, was on the sunken road 450 metres to the northeast. Although the Barrage Line started in front of the position, dropshorts prevented 15 Battalion getting close. Lumbering forward from Mouse Copse behind you, the three supporting tanks sheared across the slope, missing Pear Trench altogether. With binoculars, you can pick out the sunken road as it crosses the fields to the southeast and meets the road from Hamel in front of Vaire Wood. The German line followed the sunken road and then broke to Kidney Trench. It was located just east of Central Copse, which spills down the slope on the near side of the Hamel Road.

While 16 Battalion cleared the woods, 15 Battalion advanced this side of them and 13 Battalion along the other side. They met on the Blue Line, which ran between Hamel Wood and Accroche Wood, along

A tank, which was subsequently disabled, mopping up in Hamel. The Wolfsberg is the height above it. (AWM E02864)

Rue General John Monash and the view today. Compare the fence posts with those in the 1918 photo above.

the far spur to the Wolfsberg and down to the Somme. Imagine attacking over this exposed ground towards the Blue Line, 2,450 metres distant at the Wolfsberg, without the support of tanks. Before you leave, look westward. The tower of the Australian National Memorial rises from the far side of Hill 104 and Villers-Bretonneux can be seen to its left.

The Start Line crossed the road 400 metres south at P.14.a.5.5, which was the boundary between 15 and 16 Battalions, and ran to the right of the road before meeting it again at the junction with the D122, P.20.a.1.8, denoted by Checkpoint (**18**). 13 Battalion attacked from here, capturing 13 IR's front line at the intersection with the road from Hamel 180 metres away, where you turned for the N29 on the outward leg, and passing around the woods. **Turn left** onto the **D122** and **left again** at the Hamel road. The German line ran generally northeast, following the right side of this road for 200 metres, then crossing it to become Vaire Trench, which parallelled the left side around the front of Vaire Wood to Kidney Trench and the sunken road.

Stop at the junction of the Hamel and sunken roads (**19**), which is about 1.3 kilometres from the D122 and indicated by Checkpoint 10. 16 Battalion set up its Advance Report Centre 150 metres to the west on the Hamel road. A foot track there approximates to the line of Hun's Walk and passes the southern end of Kidney Trench, identified by the lighter patch of soil in the field, before petering out at the tip of Central Copse after 150 metres. Lance Corporal Thomas Axford of 16 Battalion won the Victoria Cross for overwhelming a machine gun post that had held up his company in this area. Pear Trench was on the crest where the sunken road crosses it. The support the two redoubts could offer each other and the natural protection the shape of the ground gave them from the Australian line are obvious.

In the opposite direction, the sunken road continues through Vaire Wood, on the other side of which it joins the minor road running down to the D122 that you passed earlier. Hun's Walk crossed this junction before continuing through Hamel Wood and across the plateau to Accroche Wood. Its line in the woods is still evident and traces of dugouts and craters abound. The cramping effect of both Vaire and Hamel Woods on tank manoeuvrability and 16 Battalion's consequent reliance on the barrage as it cleared them are easily appreciated.

On your way into Hamel, you will pass a switchback on the right after 500 metres. The Infantry Halt Line ran through it and the Germans sited several machine guns on the high ground above. Screened from observation by Hamel Wood, they had excellent enfilade fields of fire across the western end of the village and could have disrupted 43 Battalion's attack if 15 Battalion had not dealt with them. **On reaching Hamel, turn left** at the D71 and park in front of the church (**20**). The stone topped brick pillars supporting the iron railing fence on the wall across the street somehow survived the battle.

Previously la Grande Rue, the D71 through the village was renamed Rue General John Monash in 2000. You can return to the Australian Corps Memorial by turning left at the traffic island at the end of 'General John Monash Street', then right after 50 metres.

Tour Two: North of the Somme

This tour takes in the left flank of the attack, the 14 and 15 Brigade diversions and the cemeteries across the Somme. Leaving the Australian Corps Memorial (**1**), **turn right onto the D71** and stop after 500 metres at a junction where the D71 turns sharply right, a minor road goes on to Bouzencourt and a foot track heads westwards to Hamelet (**2**). An ammunition drop zone was on this junction.

The Blue Line ran down the northern slope of the Wolfsberg above you and came within 100 metres of the minor road, which shoots across the flats to the river just west of Bouzencourt, the small cluster of buildings at the road's end. The foot track was the boundary between 43 Battalion attacking Hamel and 42 Battalion, which enjoyed a relatively easy advance to the Blue Line. Notamel Wood filled the area between the track and Hamel. The tanks Bean saw crawling up the side of the Wolfsberg were probably those supporting 42 Battalion or the half of 44 Battalion that swept around the near side of the village and on up the slope to join the other half, which had moved around the far side, on the crest.

Stay on the D71 and after 1.3 kilometres you will pass the entrance to the Vallée d'Arbancourt (**3**), where 1/201 RIR and 1/202 RIR were caught assembling for the counterattack on the Wolfsberg. **Turn left onto the D42** after another kilometre and cross the Somme into Sailly-Laurette, which was behind the German line and held by the 43rd Reserve Division. At the big intersection in the village centre, take the **D223 to Sailly-le-Sec**. Just before entering the village, you

The Vallée d'Arbancourt, where heavy shelling disrupted the Germans as they assembled for their counterattack. Accroche Wood is on the skyline.

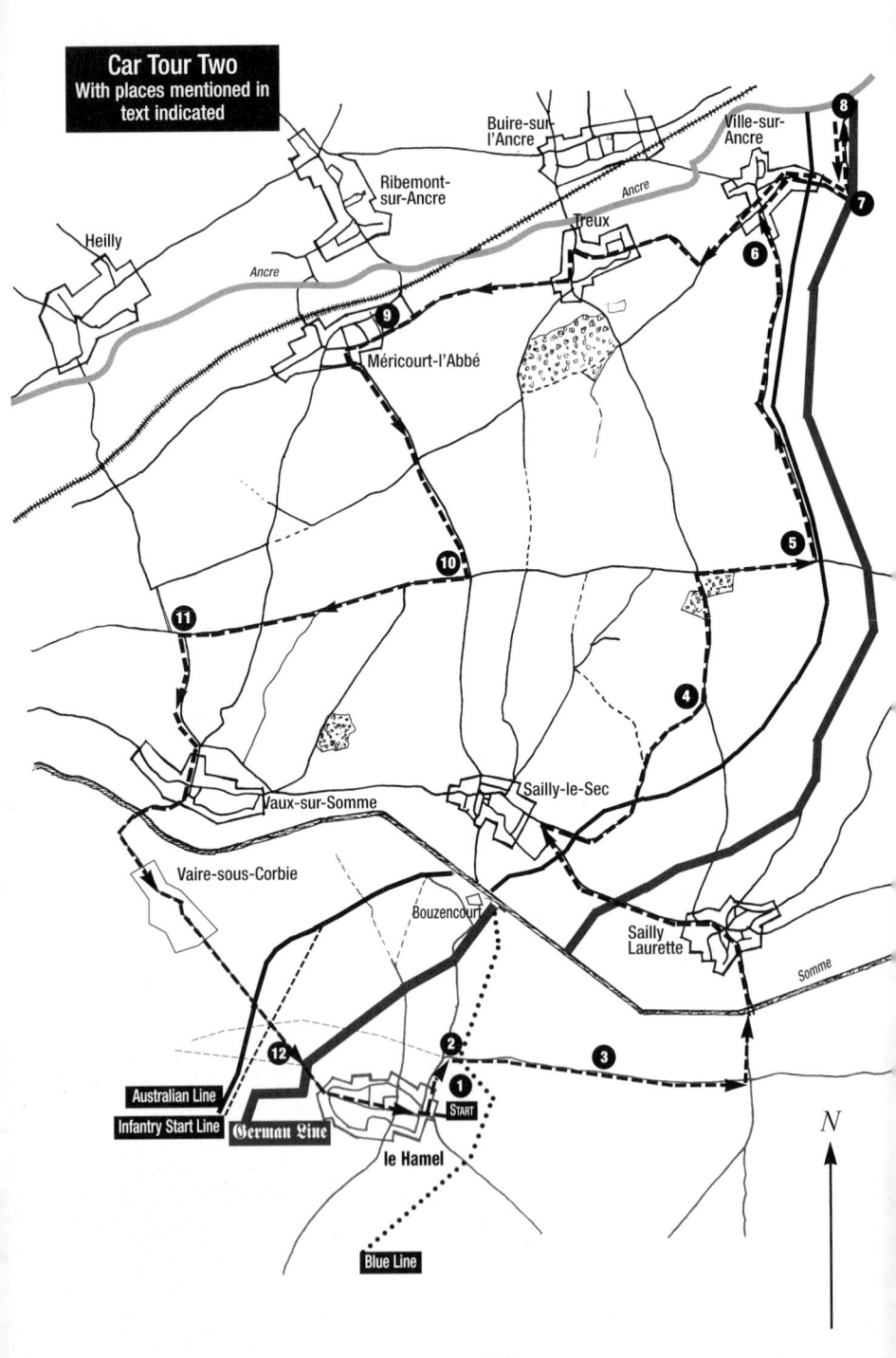

Car Tour Two
With places mentioned in text indicated

will see a cemetery on your right. At the three-way junction 250 metres beyond it, turn sharp right onto the road that heads east past the back of the cemetery. It follows the front line. After two kilometres, you will reach an **intersection at which you should turn lef**t. Park at Dive Copse Cemetery 50 metres further on (**4**).

Before the 2nd Australian Division's attack on 10 June 1918, this cemetery was a few hundred metres behind the Australian line, which ran northwards before swinging west around Morlancourt and down to Ville on the Ancre. After the attack, it was 800 metres behind and the Australians had made even greater gains near the D1, the Bray-Corbie Road, a kilometre north. 55 Battalion carried out its diversionary 'papier-maché raid' from the new line in the fields 750 metres to the southeast. Look south across the Somme and locate the Australian Corps Memorial on the Wolfsberg, Accroche Wood behind it and Hamel and Vaire Wood to the right of Accroche Wood. The Germans held this area and everything east of it. As their guns were making the 2nd Division's flank and even its rear on this side of the Somme untenable, General Rosenthal decided to hold fast until the advance on the southern bank caught up.

On reaching the D1, turn right and park at Beacon Cemetery (**5**), which is on the right after one kilometre. Virtually on the Australian line, it was named after the Brick Beacon, a tall brick chimney that rose from a ruin on the summit of the Morlancourt Ridge immediately to the southeast. The vista from the cemetery explains the tremendous tactical importance of this ground and why the Germans fought so stubbornly to hold it. Though the summit masks observation southwards, you can easily see Albert across the Ancre and the

Dugout remains in the Big Caterpillar above Ville.

Thiepval Memorial on the northern skyline. 55 Battalion carried out its costly raid across the southern shoulder 750 metres from here and the Germans held out on the summit until the night of 8-9 August. A short walk down the track on the eastern side of the cemetery opens up good views across the Somme to the Wolfsberg.

Take the minor road opposite this track, which is in poor condition initially but still passable. After 1.5 kilometres, you will see Morlancourt at the end of a narrow re-entrant on your right. Continue for another 1.5 kilometres as the road descends towards Ville on the stretch that was known as the Big Caterpillar, noting the remains of dugouts in the bank on the right. Park at the junction (**6**) with a minor road on the right and a foot track on the left, which crosses another road 250 metres west. It is the Little Caterpillar. You are on the left flank of the frontage held by 22 Battalion during 6 Brigade's attack on Ville on 19 May 1918. It captured both Caterpillars to your south, Sergeant William Ruthven winning his Victoria Cross in the Big Caterpillar about 900 metres from this location. Canberra Trench, from which 59 Battalion attacked in 15 Brigade's diversion on 4 July, ran roughly parallel to the Big Caterpillar and straddled the minor road on the right about 300 metres along, at which point that road has petered out into a foot track.

Continue into Ville, turn right onto the D120 in the village and park at the junction with the minor road on the left after a kilometre (**7**). The D120 was the boundary between 58 and 59 Battalions and the junction stood on the German front line, held by 52 IR. It ran southwest and the severe bomb fight involving Captain McDonald's company on 59 Battalion's left occurred 200 metres in that direction. The German counterattack on the opposite flank, which was held by Sergeant Little after Second Lieutenant Facey's death, struck the line 350 metres further south. Meanwhile, D Company from 58 Battalion cleared the posts strung out on the minor road opposite.

Follow this road for 650 metres to where a sharp right turn leads to Dernancourt (**8**). Shell craters and a rumpled mound on the river bank mark the site of the machine gun infested watermill that Lieutenant Thompson died capturing. As you **return to the D120**, consider the wide frontages on which the understrength Australian companies attacked and look up at the Morlancourt Heights to appreciate Brigadier General Elliott's concern for his men digging in under the German guns there. In the event, the Australian artillery smashed the Germans as they were preparing to counterattack from the feature.

Turn right onto the D120 and drive through Ville and Treux before stopping at Méricourt-l'Abbé Communal Cemetery Extension on the right about 200 metres past the junction with the D119 (**9**). Second Lieutenant Facey and Lieutenants Moore and Ranson are among those killed in the diversion who rest here. **Do not follow the D120** when it swings right 250 metres past the cemetery but **continue straight ahead for another 150 metres and turn left**. Follow this road southward to its junction with the D1, the Bray-Corbie Road, at the memorial to the 3rd Australian Division (**10**). Some accounts link this memorial to the attack on 8 August and argue that since the 3rd Division's boundary was not extended north to the Bray-Corbie Road until two days later, it would have been better placed further east. In fact, its location had nothing to do with 8 August.

The Western Front memorials to each Australian division were erected where its veterans considered their most important action took place. The 1st Division opted for Pozières; the 2nd Division selected Mt. St. Quentin; the 4th Division went for Bellenglise on the Hindenburg Line and the 5th put theirs atop the Butte in Polygon Wood. The 3rd Division veterans contemplated Messines before choosing the summit of the ridge above Sailly-le-Sec. After its dramatic arrival, masterfully planned by Monash in flickering candlelight at 1 am on 27 March 1918, the 3rd Division held the angle between the Somme and the Ancre, blocking one of the main approaches to Amiens. From then until the end of April, it relentlessly carried out peaceful penetration in this area, taking prisoners three days out of every five and becoming the most successful of all the Australian divisions in the activity. That is why its memorial stands here. The Australian Corps Memorial can be seen below Accroche Wood to the south.

The 3rd Australian Division Memorial.

Turn right onto the D1 and continue for approximately 2.2 kilometres to the intersection with a minor road on the left that runs down the ridgeline and into Vaux-sur-Somme and stop (**11**). The Australian line, Pear Trench, Vaire, Hamel and Accroche Woods, Hamel village and the Wolfsberg can all be picked out with binoculars. Bean watched the attack from this area. On 21 April 1918, Baron Manfred von Richthofen, the war's top-scoring ace and history's best-known fighter pilot, crashed in the field opposite the old brickworks with the tall chimney to your west. Who actually shot him down has always been one of the war's controversial questions but most experts today give the credit to Sergeant Cedric Popkin, a machine gunner in the 4th Australian Division. 5 Tank Brigade's forward headquarters was in a mill on the near edge of Wellcome Wood 1.3 kilometres to the southeast.

Drive into Vaux, cross the D233 and then the Somme before turning left through Vaire-sous-Corbie and taking the D71 to Hamel. Held by 202 RIR, the German line bent back from Pear Trench and swung due north to cross the D71 near the junction with the farm track that enters on the right after 1.9 kilometres (**12**). The dugout behind the beet pile that held up 43 Battalion was just to the south of the junction. Lieutenant I.G. Symons led a platoon of Americans along the road to outflank it, whereupon the position was charged from all sides. The Artillery Halt Line crossed the D71 in the village, where the road has been renamed Rue General John Monash, 400 metres further on. You can end this tour in Hamel or return to the Australian Corps Memorial by turning left on the D71 at the traffic island and then right after 50 metres.

Walk One: The Australian and German Lines, Pear and Kidney Trenches, Hamel and Vaire Woods, Hamel Village, the Blue Line

Although this walk stretches about 9.5 kilometres (six miles), the route is very gentle and you will not be carrying a heavy pack and a rifle as the infantry were in 1918! **Start** at the Australian Corps Memorial Park (**1**) by familiarising yourself with the main features on the battlefield. When you have a good mental picture of the ground, take the **road into Hamel**, which offers good views of the village. B Company from 43 Battalion with six tanks advanced towards you, clearing the houses and lanes, while A and C Companies worked back towards them after rushing around to the eastern edge of Hamel below you. The three machine guns knocked out by Lance Corporal Shaw and a supporting tank were in that area.

Turn **left** when you reach the **T-junction** with the D71, then **right after 50 metres** at the traffic island. Continue on the Rue General John Monash, the name given to the D71 as it passes through the village, to the church (**2**). You are now on the Artillery Halt Line, which crossed the D71 here. The stone topped brick pillars supporting the iron railing fence on the wall across the street were among the few parts of prewar

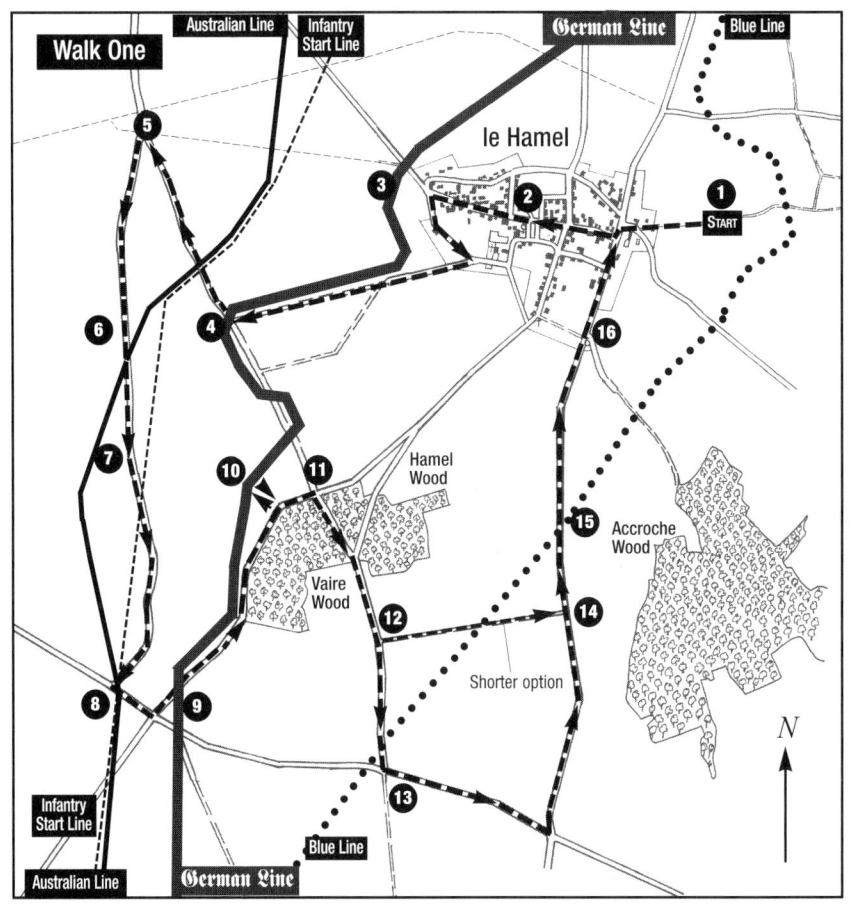

The sunken road at Pear Trench today. The bank was riddled with dugouts.

Hamel to escape destruction in the fighting. Sheltering in the cellars of the houses and in the deep dugouts that dotted the village, many soldiers from 202 RIR had their gas masks on and were completely surprised by the attack. 43 Battalion took over 300 prisoners in Hamel.

You will cross the Infantry Halt Line 200 metres further along the Rue General John Monash and reach the western tip of Hamel at a four-way intersection after another 250 metres. The beet pile that held up B Company was in the field 100 metres west (**3**). When Lieutenant Symons had outflanked it by moving along the D71, the Australians pinned down in front charged, taking the position and 40 prisoners. 202 RIR's line crossed the D71 150 metres away and headed northeast to Bouzencourt after skirting Notamel Wood, which filled the area between the village and the Cerisy-Hamelet track 400 metres to your north. Captain Moran corrected the drift when A Company of 43 Battalion lost direction in the blinding smoke here and, after a ring of the bell alerted its commander, a tank crushed a machine gun post that was holding up the advance.

Leave the D71 on the southerly road and **turn sharp right** after 300 metres. This road, which parallels the German line, becomes a farm track within 400 metres and strikes the rear of Pear Trench 400 metres further on, after which it runs through the position. The line extending northwards was attacked by C Company from 43 Battalion after Lance Corporal Shaw and an American, Corporal Zyburt, overcame a troublesome machine gun. **Continue along the track** to its junction with the sunken road. You are now at the western end of Pear Trench (**4**). It ran for almost 150 metres just the other side of the road, which was pitted with deep dugouts and littered with German corpses

An Australian infantryman's view eastwards from 15 Battalion's front line.

after the 'white flag treachery' incident, before doubling back on itself in a trench that faced Vaire and Hamel Woods and completed the pear-shaped outline that gave the redoubt its name. Several things are worth noting.

The redoubt could engage any advance towards Hamel across the low ground on either side. It was also a good example of a reverse slope position. Accentuated by the tall crops, the convex curve of the ground rendered it invisible to 15 Battalion on its Start Line 250 metres up the spur but 55 IR's Westphalians could make out their attackers against the skyline. As the line on which the barrage started tracked along the slope less than 50 metres from the sunken road, the opening salvos had to be accurate otherwise the first lift would carry the fire well beyond the position, leaving intact its trenches and the wire protecting them. Because the barrage fell short, A Company from 15 Battalion faced a frontal assault against largely untouched and concealed defences sited in depth. When the tanks failed to arrive, its task was formidable indeed. As you leave, remember Private Henry Dalziel, who won the Victoria Cross here.

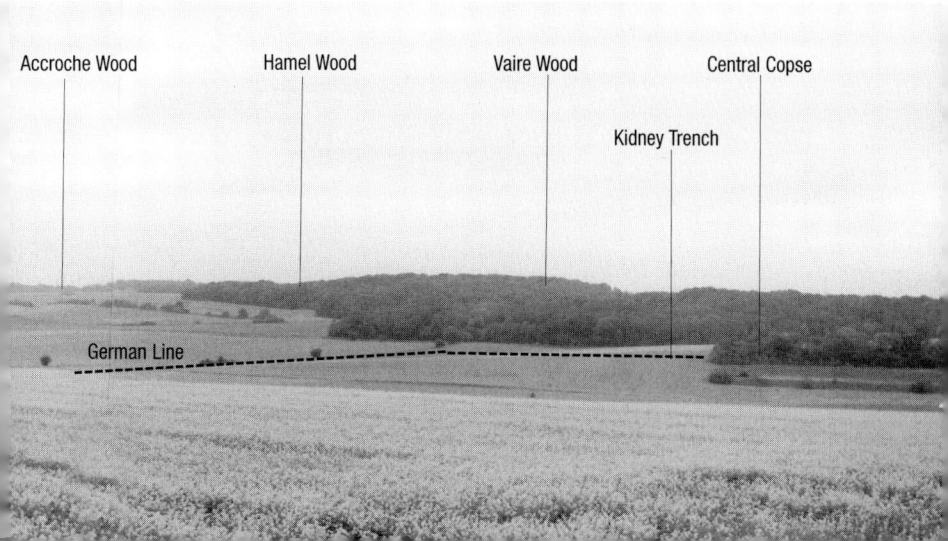

Turn right onto the sunken road. The Artillery Start Line and the boundary between 15 and 43 Battalions on the Infantry Start Line at P.8.b.1.1 crossed it respectively 50 metres and 150 metres along. Continue **down** the gentle incline for another 600 metres to a crucifix, which stands on the junction with the sealed road from Vaire to your north and the foot track from Hamel to the east (**5**). Totally devoid of cover, No Man's Land varied from 500-700 metres in front of 43 Battalion to as much as 1,400 metres for 42 Battalion assaulting on the other side of the Cerisy-Hamelet Track, which crosses the sealed road 100 metres northwards. These distances made surprise and attacking in darkness essential. The open ground, unchanged over the years, was perfect for tanks.

   Take the **sealed road up the spur**, stop after 900 metres at the sign for Checkpoint 7 and climb the roadside pile of chalk ballast that you saw from the Wolfsberg. You are now at P.8.c.5.4, where 4 Brigade's front line, held by 15 Battalion, crossed the road (**6**). Pear Trench was 450 metres to the northeast, hidden, like the sunken road, by the convex slope. The shape of the ground and the poor light defeated the three tanks supporting A Company on the left of 15 Battalion. They started from the area of Mouse Copse behind you but missed Pear Trench. Using binoculars, you can see the sunken road emerging in the fields to the southeast and heading up the slope to meet the road from Hamel at Vaire Wood. The German line followed it from Pear Trench but broke across the slope to Kidney Trench at the eastern end of Central Copse, which appears as an untidy extension of the wood.

   Crowning the Wolfsberg above Hamel 2,450 metres to the east, the Australian Corps Memorial signifies the Blue Line, which you can follow towards Accroche Wood. The suitability of the intervening ground for tanks is striking yet again. Look westward to see the tower of the Australian National Memorial rising from the far side of Hill 104 and the spires of Villers-Bretonneux to its left. You can also see Bouzencourt and Vaire on the Somme, which places this location roughly in the centre of the attack, making it a good place to let your imagination take you back to the early hours of 4 July 1918.

   Lying out on the Start Line in the crops 100 metres to the east, you feel clammy in the damp mist. You are thankful that the racket from the FE2b's overhead is drowning out the noise of the tanks moving up towards Mouse Copse. Your heart stops when a misdropped parachute flare turns night into day but begins beating again when the German line, which you know is a few hundred metres over the crest, does not stir. When the harassing fire starts at 3.02 am, you hope the occupants

The German line from Kidney Trench.

put their gas masks on.

Eight minutes later, the sky behind you disappears in a continuous white flash and a few seconds later the ground in front of you erupts in a sea of red flame. The concussion rattles every bone in your body and clods of earth rain down like giant hailstones. Your eyes water and you gasp for breath as the smoke from the shellbursts transforms the mist into a foul smelling ground-level cloud. Multi-coloured SOS rockets rise from the German line in a kaleidoscopic display and the long lines of glowing tracer from the machine gun barrage add to the colour. Your ears are aching from the din and you barely hear the whistle that tells you to head into the line of fire. But you know it's time to go anyway. You hug the barrage, pray that no rounds drop short and hope that the tanks are on their way.

Continue for another 400 metres to P.14.a.5.5, which was the boundary between 15 and 16 Battalions (**7**). The Start Line crossed the road near this point and ran on its right to the junction with the D122 at P.20.a.1.8, identified by Checkpoint 8 (**8**). 13 Battalion's left flank was in the field 90 metres north of the junction at P.14.c.2.0 and the right stretched 360 metres south of it to P.20.a.0.0. For the German view, **turn left** onto the D122 and **left again** at the Hamel/Villers-Bretonneux road after 180 metres, which puts you on the line held by 13 and 15 IR (**9**). As this intersection was under the Barrage Line, the post in the quarry on the left of the road vanished. D Company from 13 Battalion passed over it and had a relatively trouble free advance to the southern tip of Vaire Wood 650 metres away. The rest of the battalion followed.

Take the Hamel road. The German line followed the right side for 200 metres and then crossed over to become Vaire Trench, which skirted around the front of Vaire Wood. About a kilometre from the D122 and just before a sharp bend, a foot track enters on the left. 16 Battalion established its Advanced Report Centre on this junction,

P.14.b.6.1, which is also where Hun's Walk entered Vaire Wood. Head along the track, which roughly follows the line of Hun's Walk to the tip of Central Copse, the clump of scraggy trees 150 metres distant.

On reaching Central Copse, you will be standing at the southern end of Kidney Trench (**10**), a double line of trenches with posts in between that stretched 180 metres northeast and 90 metres rearwards. It enfiladed the line to the north, which met the sunken road 250 metres away and followed it up the far slope to Pear Trench on the crest. Lance Corporal Thomas Axford's VC exploit during D Company's assault on Kidney Trench ensured its fall, thereby removing the clear threat it posed to the flank of 15 Battalion's attack.

Return to the Hamel Road. After 150 metres, **turn right** at the sunken road and **enter Vaire Wood** at Checkpoint 10 (**11**). Having cleared Vaire Trench, 16 Battalion swept through the wood, which was not as dense then as it is now. Nevertheless, the trees hampered the six supporting tanks and held the smoke and mist, which made signalling them difficult. Though the tanks did useful work, the infantry's best asset was the barrage. Firing their Lewis Guns from the hip, they drove the Germans into it. Traces of shell holes and dugouts can be seen either side of the sunken road, which joins a sealed road near the tree line after 250 metres. You can also pick up the line of Hun's Walk, which ran diagonally through the wood on your right and passed through this junction on its way to Accroche Wood. Many Germans withdrew along it.

Continue on the sealed road to the farm track that enters on the left 300 metres from the tree line (**12**). The centre of the expanse bounded by the road and the two sides of the wood to its west was the site of a carrier tank dumping point, while the area around you served as an ammunition drop zone. Both were set up for 13 Battalion, which assaulted towards you between the wood and the D122 500 metres south. D Company dug in from the southern corner of Vaire Wood to the D122. A and B Companies moved through it and made a double wheel north and east around the tree line and across the road until they were stopped by machine guns in a concealed trench in the field between the road and the wood. Captain George Marper was badly wounded while summoning a tank to deal with them. The support line dug by C Company of 14 Battalion passed diagonally through your location.

The road that runs north to Hamel is 750 metres along the farm track. **Alternatively**, if you are feeling energetic and don't mind hiking a couple of extra kilometres, continue southward to the D122, which

The Villers-Bretonneux plateau across which 6 Brigade attacked on the left flank. The town is on the right and the N29 forms the horizon.

will put you squarely on the Villers-Bretonneux plateau (**13**). The Blue Line crossed the D122 100 metres west of the intersection at P.21.a.4.0, the boundary between 4 and 6 Brigades, before passing in front of Accroche Wood. Pivoting on its right flank, C Company from 13 Battalion swung its left flank forward to link up with B Company in the fields 400 metres northeast of your location.

In the opposite direction, the Blue Line ran southwestwards to the N29, which meant that 6 Brigade had to execute a similar manoeuvre. Attacking along the D122, 21 Battalion advanced almost a kilometre, five times as far as 23 Battalion's right flank on the highway. Ironically, 23 Battalion had the toughest fighting, with D Company encountering stubborn resistance that also troubled 25 Battalion's diversionary attack alongside. The post captured by Sergeant Ham and the eight survivors of B Company 25 Battalion and held against 3/137 IR's counterattacks, was just the other side of the N29. Although the Australians gratefully took over well-constructed defences on the right flank, many of the trenches in 6 Brigade's area were flimsy. Some were being used as latrines.

The flat and open terrain towards the N29 explains why it was the target area for most of the 9.2-inch shelling that created craters for the infantry to use as cover. As the ground also favoured tanks more than anywhere else on the attacking frontage, they had the hardest fighting in this area and earned lavish praise from all ranks of 6 Brigade. The barrage and smokescreen were flawless. Monash's concept of a combined arms attack in which mechanical resources helped the infantry forward came closest to perfection here. Note how much more depth the attack gave the Australians on the Villers-Bretonneux plateau.

Head east on the D122. You will cross the Protective Barrage Line after 270 metres. **Turn left** onto the Hamel road 430 metres further on and **stop at the farm track** that enters from the left 900 metres later (**14**). It is the eastern end of the one at which you paused shortly after exiting Vaire Wood. Made up of trenches scattered either side of the road, the German support line ran through this area, as did Ration Row, a communications sap that headed northwest into Hamel Wood. It crossed the Blue Line in the field 200 metres to the west at a gap that should have been held by A Company 13 Battalion. Digging the support line behind A Company, Lieutenant Rule's platoon had a nervous time when they rushed forward to fill it. Lieutenant Ramsay Wood was also sniped there.

The Blue Line and Hun's Walk, which linked Hamel and Accroche Woods and 13 and 55 IR used as an escape route, crossed the road 300 metres north at the sign for Checkpoint 13 (**15**). It also marks the boundary between 13 and 15 Battalions. The Blue Line passed in front of Accroche Wood on its way to the Wolfsberg and the Protective Barrage Line ran just inside the wood. Tanks and infantry parties went beyond it to mop up even as the barrage fell. Consequently, many Australians felt afterwards that the Blue Line should have been further east but Monash would not risk a potentially stiff fight in and around Accroche Wood at the end of an already long advance. The nearness of the wood exemplifies his conception of Hamel as a limited attack.

Walking down the hill towards Hamel, you will pass the northeastern corner of Hamel Wood on your left. The Germans in the wood made their last stand there. They also sited several machine guns along the terraced slope that overlooks the Hamel/Villers-Bretonneux Road below you. Masked by the wood and holding the western end of the village in enfilade, these guns were a threat to 43 Battalion's attack until 15 Battalion overran them on its way to linking up with 13

Hamel from the site of the Chapelle St. Roche. An Australian patrol is on the road at left. (AWM E02665)

The same view today.

Battalion on Hun's Walk.

On the right of the road, and signposted as Checkpoint 14, 500 metres from Hamel, the Chapelle St. Roche (**16**) is a good vantage point from which to ponder the attack on 202 RIR in the village and on the Wolfsberg. While 43 Battalion cleared Hamel, 44 Battalion split with six tanks either side of it and linked up on the Blue Line, which crossed the Wolfberg and passed along its southern shoulder 600 metres behind your location. 44 Battalion met 15 Battalion in that vicinity at P.10.d.7.3. The trench that pinned down 15 Battalion extended towards Accroche Wood on the high ground behind you. Fifty Germans and 27 machine guns were captured after a tank drove along it.

D Company from 14 Battalion took another 15 prisoners while digging the northern end of the support line immediately east of the chapel. Ammunition drop zones and dumping points for carrier tanks were established either side of the chapel between Hamel Wood and the Wolfsberg, to which you should now return. But you may care to stop in the village to refresh yourself at the café in the Rue John Monash. You probably deserve it!

WALK TWO: THE SOMME FLANK

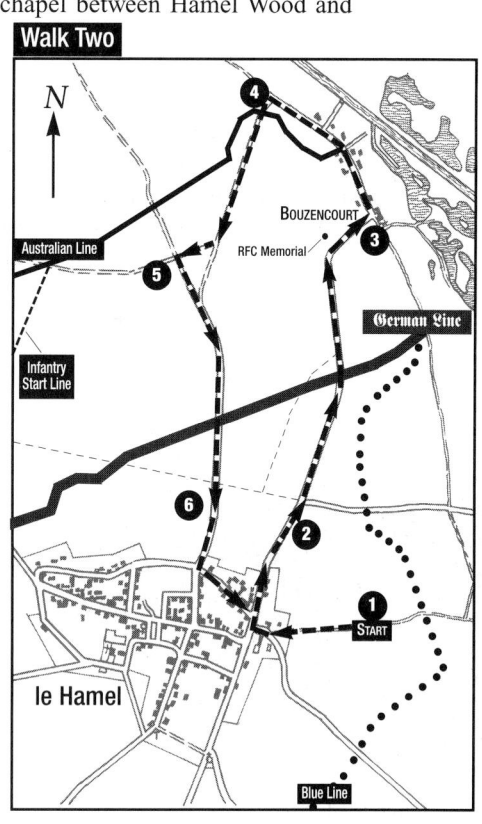

This walk of four kilometres covers the largely ignored Somme flank. You can start from the Australian Corps Memorial (**1**), where the bird's eye view of the terrain helps to set the various parts of the walk within the overall context of the battlefield, or in Hamel itself. Head **north out of the village** on the D71 and stop where it swings right towards Cerisy and a minor road goes on to Bouzencourt (**2**). The site of an ammunition drop zone, this junction was roughly midway between the Blue Line, which crossed the D71 180 metres to the east after running down the northern shoulder of the Wolfsberg, and the Artillery Halt Line, which passed over the foot track that leads westwards to Hamelet. This track was the boundary between 43 Battalion attacking Hamel and 42 Battalion extending the line to the Somme.

Stay on the minor road. The Artillery Halt Line followed the foot track that parallels the road and enters on the left after 550 metres, where the German line also crossed it. Several German trenches seamed the fields in between and a carrier tank dumping point was located in them. You will reach **Bouzencourt (3)**, such as it is, 550 metres further on, where the road turns sharp left at a chapel and follows the river. A memorial to Captain Francis Mond and Lieutenant Edgar Martyn of 57 Squadron RAF, who crashed here on 5 May 1918 is on the left 150 metres short of the bend. Sailly-le-Sec on the opposite bank was just behind the Australian line, which headed northeast up the slope to Morlancourt and Ville-sur-Ancre. After 600 metres, a track leads from the road into a camping ground but you should **take the road on the left (4)**, which soon peters out into a farm track. The Australian line crossed near this point.

The memorial to Captain Mond and Lieutenant Martyn.

Continue along the **farm track** and **turn right** after 500 metres onto **another track that skirts the southern edge of a small orchard** before meeting a north-south farm track at the western corner **(5)**. The extreme left of the attack at P.3.b.2.9 was 500 metres due west of this junction. In 1918 the area was wooded and lingering German Blue Cross gas discomfited A Company from 42 Battalion on the Start Line. Fortunately, the Germans were over a kilometre distant and could not hear the Australians sneezing. Arriving on time at 3.14 am, the tanks hugged the barrage and H.S. Shapcott vividly described the scene as they crushed the German posts. Now head towards Hamel on the north-south farm track, which becomes a sealed road after 100 metres. The Infantry Halt Line and the German front line both crossed it 600 metres along. On reaching the Cerisy-Hamelet track shortly afterwards **(6)**, you will have covered 42 Battalion's attacking frontage.

43 Battalion attacked south of this track and Notamel Wood extended from it to the northern rim of Hamel. The German line crossed the western edge of the wood, where A Company ran into stiff resistance after losing direction in the thick smoke. Its commander, Captain Moran, regained his bearings when he saw the treetops

highlighted by the bursting shells of the barrage and got his men back on course. A tank was summoned to wipe out a troublesome machine gun nearby. One half of 44 Battalion passed through this area to join the other half, which had swept around the southern side of Hamel, for the attack on the Wolfsberg. The tanks Bean saw grinding up its slopes were those supporting the northern half of 44 Battalion or the ones with 42 Battalion on the shoulder above the Somme. When you reach Hamel, turn right at the Rue General John Monash (D71) and follow the signs back to the Australian Corps Memorial.

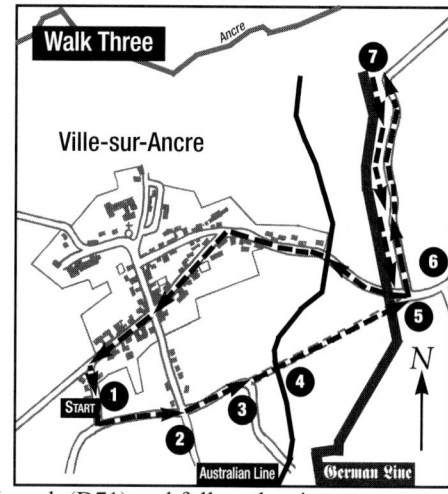

Walk Three: The Big and Little Caterpillars and 15 Brigade's Diversionary Attack at Ville-sur-Ancre

Approximately four kilometres long, this walk traces the operations of 58 and 59 Battalions during 15 Brigade's diversionary attack on the Ancre at Ville. It starts at the **Ville-sur-Ancre Communal Cemetery and Military Extension**, just off the D120 immediately west of the village and the site of a German post in 1918 (**1**). A foot track crosses the sunken road 50 metres south of the cemetery. The sunken road was the Little Caterpillar, while the foot track formed the boundary between 21 and 22 Battalions in the attack on 19 May. **Head east for 250 metres** along it to another sunken road, the Big Caterpillar (**2**). 22 Battalion assaulted across both Caterpillars, the banks of which were lined with German posts. Their remains are still visible. Sergeant Ruthven won the Victoria Cross at the Big Caterpillar a kilometre to the south.

After crossing the Big Caterpillar, continue on the sealed road, which is also riddled with traces of dugouts, and then the foot track. It carries on in the original northeasterly direction when the road swings south after 250 metres (**3**). Canberra Trench, from which 59 Battalion attacked, crossed the track 100 metres past this point (**4**). Now walk another **400 metres to the junction with the D120** (**5**), from where the German line, held by 52 IR, ran southwest across the fields. The left platoon of B Company entered it in the area of the junction and began

The remains of the mill on the Ancre where Lieutenant Thompson died.

bombing inwards. Wire entanglements concealed by the crops held up the centre, whose survivors joined the right platoon that was bombing up the trench towards you. Lewis Gunners around your location broke a German counterattack. The barricades defended by Second Lieutenant Facey and Sergeant Little from A Company were 550 metres along the trench.

Before leaving, look up at the Morlancourt Heights. Brigadier General Elliott's anxiety about consolidating in daylight below the guns located on this dominating position was understandable. A well-preserved Demarcation Stone, showing the limit of the German advance in 1918, stands 100 metres east where the road to Morlancourt leaves the D120 (**6**).

The German line to the Ancre consisted of a few posts scattered along the road to Dernancourt opposite, which was on one of the driest parts of the surrounding flats. **Take this road and stop 650 metres** along at the abrupt right turn near the river (**7**). Standing on the bank are the remains of the heavily defended mill where Lieutenant Thompson was killed. The millrace passes a pitted mound that is littered with shattered bricks from the foundations of the workings. Part of a millstone juts from the field around it, which is pock-marked by overgrown shell craters.

As you walk **back to the D120**, imagine D Company from 58 Battalion attacking along this frontage with 80 men. Return to your starting point at the cemetery by the way you have come or by continuing on the D120 through Ville. The route though the village is longer but holds out the prospect of a refreshing drink. You may well appreciate it!

SELECT BIBLIOGRAPHY

I relied heavily in the writing of this guide on primary sources held by the Australian War Memorial. They comprise, firstly, the Operational Records Files for the Fourth Army, Australian Corps and 4th Australian Division, which contain all the instructions, orders and reports relevant to the Hamel attack, including for supporting arms and services such as 5 Tank Brigade and 5 Brigade RAF, and secondly, war diaries at army, corps, division, brigade and battalion levels. The files I found most useful, as well as personal manuscripts, are listed in the notes at the end of each chapter.

The following secondary sources describe the battle or specific aspects of it:
1. R. Austin, *Forward Undeterred. The History of the 23rd Battalion 1915-1918* (Slouch Hat Publications, 1998).
2. C.E.W. Bean, *Anzac to Amiens*, (AWM, 1968).
3. C.E.W. Bean, *The Official History of Australia in the War of 1914-1918. V. The AIF in France During the Main German Offensive, 1918* (Angus & Robertson, 1937).
4. C.E.W. Bean, *The Official History of Australia in the War of 1914-1918. VI. The AIF in France During the Allied Offensive, 1918* (Angus & Robertson, 1942).
5. R.A. Beaumont, 'Hamel, 1918: A Study in Military-Political Interaction' in *Military Affairs*, Vol XXXI, No. 1, Spring 1967.
6. R.G.S. Bidwell, *Gunners at War* (Arms and Armour Press, 1970).
7. G. Blaxland, *Amiens 1918* (W.H. Allen, 1981).
8. P. J. Campbell, *The Ebb and Flow of Battle* (OUP, 1979).
9. F.M. Cutlack, *The Official History of Australia in the War of 1914-1918. The Australian Flying Corps* (Angus & Robertson, 1923).
10. F.M. Cutlack (ed), *War Letters of General Monash* (Angus & Robertson, 1934).
11. R. Donelley, *Black Over Blue. The 25th Battalion AIF at War 1915-18,* (USQ Press, 1997).
12. J.E. Edmonds, *Military Operations: France and Belgium 1918. III. May-July* (McMillan, 1939).
13. H. Essame, *The Battle for Europe 1918* (Charles Scribner's Sons, 1972).
14. J.F.C. Fuller, *Memoirs of an Unconventional Soldier* (Nicholson & Watson, 1936).
15. J. Laffin, *The Battle of Hamel* (Kangaroo Press, 1999).
16. F.B. Maurice (Ed.), *The Life of Lord Rawlinson of Trent* (Cassell, 1928).
17. C. Longmore, *The Old Sixteenth* (16 Battalion Association, 1929).
18. M. and M. Middlebrook, *The Somme Battlefields* (Viking, 1991).
19. G.D. Mitchell, *Backs to the Wall* (Angus & Roberston, 1937).
20. J. Monash, *The Australian Victories in France in 1918* (Hutchinson, 1920).
21. P.A. Pedersen, *Monash as Military Commander* (Melbourne University Press, 1985).
22. J.J. Pershing, *My Experiences in the World War* (Harper & Row, 1932).
23. R. Prior and T. Wilson, *Command on the Western Front* (Blackwell, 1992).
24. E.J. Rule, *Jacka's Mob* (Angus & Robertson, 1933).
25. E.K.G. Sixsmith, *British Generalship in the Twentieth Century* (Arms and Armour Press, 1970).
26. J. Terraine, *Douglas Haig. The Educated Soldier* (Hutchinson, 1963).
27. J. Terraine, *To Win a War* (Sidgwick & Jackson, 1978).
28. N. Wanliss, *The History of the Fourteenth Battalion AIF* (Arrow, 1929).
29. T.A. White, *The Fighting Thirteenth* (Tyrell's, 1934).

SELECTIVE INDEX

Accroche Wood, 22, 41-3, 54, 77, 81, 93-95, 97, 130-2, 134, 139-40, 143, 145, 150, 152-3, 155

American Expeditionary Force
33 Div, 58, 59, 111
131 Regt, 59, 60, 70, 79
132 Regt, 59, 70, 71, 74
Australian Corps Memorial Park, 6, 10, 21, 127-8, 130-2, 141, 143, 145-6, 150, 155, 157

Australian Imperial Force
Australian Corps, 7, 18, 14, 30, 33, 36, 39, 43, 100
2 Div, 33-35, 41, 47, 122, 143, 145
3 Div, 33-34, 36, 37-9, 41, 47, 107, 122, 125
4 Div, 30, 33, 35, 36, 41, 43, 47-8, 64, 110, 117, 145, 146
5 Div, 33, 36, 41, 55, 100, 123, 145
4 Bde, 37, 47, 50, 64-5, 67, 69, 81-2, 92, 96, 106, 109, 116, 130, 132, 134, 137, 139, 150, 153
6 Bde, 47, 50, 54, 69, 86-7,94, 98, 106, 109, 132, 134-5, 144, 153
7 Bde, 56, 105, 109, 132, 135
11 Bde, 47, 50, 63, 82, 85, 87, 89, 92, 96, 97-8, 109, 130, 138
14 Bde, 55, 123, 141
15 Bde, 29, 103, 105, 108, 109, 123, 141, 144, 157
13 Bn, 47, 58, 70, 81-2, 92-4, 96, 100, 115, 118, 123, 126, 134, 135, 139-40, 151-5
14 Bn, 47, 57, 60, 69, 92-4, 96, 123, 134, 152, 155
15 Bn, 47, 70, 71-7, 82, 85, 91-2, 94-5, 98, 113, 115, 127, 132, 134, 139-40, 149-52, 154-5
16 Bn, 47, 77-81, 82, 94, 115, 139-40, 151-2
21 Bn, 47, 64, 86, 123, 157
22 Bn, 34, 144, 157
23 Bn, 47, 64, 69, 86-7, 98, 105, 135, 153
25 Bn, 56, 105, 113, 135, 153
41 Bn., 47, 63, 87, 89
42 Bn, 47, 60, 70, 85, 88, 141, 156, 157
43 Bn, 47, 70, 82-5, 88-9, 98-99, 132, 139-141, 146, 148-9, 154-6
44 Bn, 47, 85, 89-91, 107, 126, 132, 141, 155, 157

55 Bn, 55, 100-1, 126, 131, 143-4
58 Bn, 103, 126, 144, 157-8
59 Bn, 104, 125, 144, 157
3 Sqn, AFC, 55, 92, 96
Axford, Lcpl. T., VC. 78-9, 124, 140, 152

British Army
Fourth Army, 8, 20, 27, 42, 58, 64, 113
5 Tank Bde, 9, 42, 61, 146
8 Tank Bn., 49, 50, 137

Bouzencourt, 21, 46, 82, 88, 131, 138-9, 141, 148, 150, 155-6

Cemeteries
Adelaide, 122-3, 136
Aubigny British, 123
Beacon, 123, 143-4
Crucifix Corner, 94, 123-4, 136
Daours Communal Extension, 79, 124
Dive Copse, 124-5, 143
Fouilloy Communal, 125
Méricourt-l'Abbé Communal Extension, 105, 125, 130, 145
Villers-Bretonneux Military and Australian National Memorial, 10, 21, 125-6, 130, 137, 139, 150

Courage, Brig. Gen. A., 42, 43-6, 50, 53, 115-7, 120

Dalziel, Pte. H., VC. 73-4, 139, 149

Elliott, Brig. Gen. H.E., 29, 55, 103, 105, 144, 158

German Army
13 Div, 25-7, 77, 106
43 Reserve Div, 25, 27, 98, 106, 107, 141
54 Reserve Div, 108
107 Division, 25-6, 28, 34, 103, 108
108 Division, 26, 28, 105, 106
13 IR, 26, 94, 106, 109, 134-5, 140, 151
15 IR, 26, 86-7, 106, 109, 135, 151
55 IR, 26, 77, 106, 109, 134, 144, 149
52 RIR, 25, 103-4, 108-9, 157
137 IR, 26, 105, 109, 113, 135, 153
201 RIR, 107, 141
202 RIR, 25, 84, 88-9, 98, 100,

106-7, 109, 113, 130, 132, 141, 146, 148, 155

Haig, F. M. Sir D., 29, 30, 32, 34, 41, 47-8, 55, 58-9, 64-5, 111
Hamel, 9, 13, 15, 21-2, 25, 35, 41, 43-4, 46, 50, 53, 56, 74, 77-8, 82, 84-5, 87-90, 98-9, 106, 113, 125, 127, 129, 130-2, 139-41, 145-6, 148-50, 152, 154-7
Hamel Wood, 21-2, 24-5, 43, 50, 77-82, 85, 92, 94, 113, 130, 132, 134-5, 139-40, 143, 145, 148, 154-5

Kidney Trench, 21-2, 23, 77-81, 130, 139-40, 150, 152

Monash, Gen. Sir J., 7, 8, 14, 36-40, 41-67, 69, 86, 90, 109-11, 115, 118, 119-20, 128, 145
Morlancourt, 10, 28, 34, 35, 41, 49, 122, 143-4, 156, 158

Pear Trench, 21-3, 26, 42, 44, 46, 50, 70-7, 82, 94, 116, 130, 139-40, 145-6, 148-52

Rawlinson, Gen. Sir H., 20, 41-3, 45, 47, 49, 55, 58-9, 64, 118

Royal Air Force
5 Bde, 55, 98, 118
9 Sqn, 55, 96
101 Sqn, 56, 65, 67, 69

Rule, Lt. E., 57, 60, 68-9, 93-4, 134, 154
Ruthven, Sgt. W., VC. 34-5, 144, 157

Sinclair-MacLagan, Maj. Gen. Sir H.E., 36, 41, 43, 47-50, 55, 57, 111

Vaire Wood, 21-3, 25-6, 35, 41, 43, 46, 50, 71, 77-82, 94, 113, 124, 130, 132, 135, 139-40, 143, 145, 149, 151-2, 154
Villers-Bretonneux, 10-11, 20-1, 28, 33, 41, 43, 47, 94, 122, 123, 125-6, 135-6, 139, 150
Ville-sur-Ancre, 21, 34, 55, 103, 105, 122, 125, 143-5, 156, 157-8

Wolfsberg, 21-3, 43, 82, 88, 89-91, 98-100, 106-7, 113, 118, 123, 127, 130-2, 139, 141, 143-4, 145, 150, 155-7